THE *Feminine* CODES

Your Essential Guide to Unlocking Your Inner Power

BELINDA M CLARKE

"The privilege of a lifetime is to become who you truly are."

— CG Jung

The Feminine Codes: *Your Essential Guide to Unlocking Your Inner Power*

ISBN: 978-1-7384263-0-0

First published in Great Britain in 2023 through Amazon self-publishing service Kindle Direct Publishing

Disclaimer
To protect the identities of parties that do not wish to be named or identified; some names have been changed by the author.

This book contains general health and wellbeing information based on the experience of the author. It is not meant as medical advice, diagnosis or treatment, and you must not rely on the information in this book as an alternative or substitute to medical advice from your doctor or other professional healthcare provider. If you have any concerns or questions regarding your health or that of your children or adults within your care, you should seek advice from your doctor or other professional healthcare provider.

To the extent that you rely on any information in this book, you assume all risks involved in such reliance.

Produced by samanthahoughton.co.uk

Dedication

I dedicate this book, The Feminine Codes, to you, dear reader, for breaking away from the crowd and being the way-shower you truly are. Enjoy the journey to your authentic feminine, and thank you for allowing me to guide you. I hope the pages speak to you as much as they talk to me.

Table of Contents

Foreword

I thought about asking Reese Witherspoon, Fearne Cotton or Shonda Rhimes to write a witty and 'of the moment' foreword for The Feminine Codes. They are all incredibly talented and creative women in their own right, and they go out of their way to stick their heads above the parapet to convey their messages of equality.

Then I realised that I don't personally know any of them and the time it will take to get past their gatekeepers will take far too long. I haven't got that amount of time. The time is now. The recent hit movie Barbie felt like a catalyst for rapid change. The movie's message is that Barbie and Ken are only truly happy when they achieve a balance of both masculine and feminine. I don't have time to wait. Also, combined, the likelihood of my request actually reaching them was extremely low.

As I was listening to Shonda's The Year of Yes, a brilliantly written and inspirational book - I took the lead from Rhonda and decided to write it myself! Yes, I know it's not the conventional way to write a foreword for a book, but then again, I'm not your conventional kind of girl!

You see, I am a disrupter. I always have been and always will be. It's quite a bold statement, but it's true. I disrupt the status quo. I was a punk at thirteen and got pregnant on purpose at fourteen. I've always questioned things, yet this balances nicely with my authentic nurturing side. I also ask lots of questions. It's my job to ask questions. I get paid to ask people questions and challenge their comfort zone. Where I'm from, the UK, people call this awkward. I have been awkward all my life. I know this as my family of origin has always referred to me as 'the awkward one'. The awkward one that asks lots of questions and needs to know why I'm doing something before I actually do it. And awkward because I won't just do as anyone tells me. But that's okay with me. If people see my asking uncomfortable questions as awkward, so be it. I'm awkward. I'm also very compassionate.

I also know what I like and have no qualms in politely letting people know this. For example, suppose I've ordered a cocktail and feel there isn't enough fresh lime juice. In that case, I will politely ask the bartender for some more, regardless of whether the recipe says it has enough. I'm not going to drink something that is okay when it could taste so much better to me if I only need to speak up and ask. This can be difficult for many women as society and caregivers have raised them to comply and not make a fuss.

I am a disrupter. I am awkward. I am particular. I am a nurturer. I am compassionate. I am authentic.

Now you know this about me, it makes sense that I've written a book about helping women awaken their sleepy feminine

DNA to balance their already established masculine mindset and reactions harmoniously. I've never felt okay with the man taking the lead; jobs for the boys or women are weak. But these messages have been cemented into the very foundation of our lives. At first, I rebelled, thinking I could do anything a man could. Then I started to realise it wasn't about them and us. I didn't need to compete for equality; I needed to balance my inner masculine and feminine to feel my equality instead of competing with myself!

My masculine won the competition for a long time until my realisation in my thirties woke me up to awakening my sleepy feminine DNA and giving her space to stretch out, breathe and find her voice. The discovery that I had been operating from a clearly overly masculine perspective in everything I did and possessed hardly any feminine skills or tools stopped me in my tracks. It was such a light bulb moment that it's etched on my brain as a memory, like a tombstone, but for my life, not my death. It woke me up with a huge jolt, so much so that I quit my job and marriage the same week.

This revelation led me to reassess my life - to retrain for a new career and meet my soulmate and best friend. I wanted to live my purpose and begin sharing my life's work - to help women step into their feminine power and balance it harmoniously with their masculine to act and react with the appropriate tool for that moment.

Femininity is about embracing the feminine qualities of Creativity, Compassion, Communication, Confidence, Care, Connection and Collaboration as strengths. Embodying the feminine takes awareness, desire, practice, repetition and learning new ways, as it's not just about being positive, women's circles, love and light and what you wear. Femininity is about being vulnerable, brave and bold enough to stick your head above the parapet and question the societal norm that swings heavily in favour of the masculine and the automatic programming of the patriarchal world.

The Feminine Codes will help, guide and support you to question whether you are happy with the global narrative. Do you have enough tools to act and respond to everyday situations with a balanced and complete toolbox of techniques? Are you in alignment with both your feminine and masculine, or are you a wolf in sheep's clothing, pretending?

Are you ready to dig for gold and the integrity to become who you truly are? A whole and balanced you.

Much love,
Belinda M Clarke,
October 2023.

Why I Wrote This Book

We are entering into a new era of being. A period that's moving away from doing, doing, doing, more, more, more, push, push, push and working harder.

This new era is one of balance, letting things go, allowing and trusting. A heart-centred, instead of head-lead, way of being in this world. A way to live equally and harmoniously with both our feminine and masculine sides, drawing on whichever we need at any moment in response to that situation. These are new and exciting times to be alive and live through. You have the opportunity to be part of this new era.

The Feminine Codes introduces a way of thinking and being in this world that is more inclusive. One that deviates from the ultra-masculine path of thought imposed by wealthy, white male intellectuals to underpin all 'right' thinking, which society implemented many moons ago but is now outdated and defunct.

Femininity means many things to many people. Everyone has their own idea about what femininity is or is not. I'm not here to enter that specific debate. There is much, much more to expressing your feminine side than looks alone. It's not how our patriarchal society portrays femininity or how the media promotes it. This is a feminine model construct that doesn't speak to your heart. Patriarchal society created it for power, control and manipulation.

Being feminine isn't about what you wear or how much lip gloss you apply. It's a mindset that consciously and subconsciously influences all your thoughts, patterns and actions. A mindset that many women are missing out on.

This book introduces you to an authentic way of being feminine. It's the blueprint that helped me to go from living in my overdeveloped masculine in all aspects of my life - work, home, family, and social - to accessing my deeply hidden feminine in all her wonderful and unique glory. It helped me breathe life into my lost feminine side that had been neglected and discarded, brought her back to life and transformed how I started to think and act for the better.

I will introduce you to the seven codes I developed and used to unlock my femininity and live a happy, healthy, balanced life. These seven codes are my life's work. For the past two decades I have helped hundreds of women discover their hidden inner feminine side; now it's your turn.

Are your ways of being in this life not working for you anymore?

Do you find yourself unable to fix problematic situations?

Would you like to discover new useful tools to remedy solutions easily?

Are you ready to unlock your feminine codes?

Your journey to discovering your feminine power starts here. These are the key features that you will learn from The Feminine Codes:

- *Discover the three signs that show you're disconnected from your **Feminine Power**.*
- *Learn how to balance your Feminine **and** Masculine sides.*
- *Get clarity on your unique **superpower** and how to use it.*
- *Equip yourself with **essential tools** to feel energised and fulfilled for life.*

Much love and happiness,

Belinda x

Acknowledgements

This book would not be here were it not for the brilliant Samantha Houghton, my book coach and mentor, throughout the whole process. Sam has kept me on the straight and narrow, focused at all times and incredibly supportive of my work. I literally couldn't have asked for a better guide; thank you, Sam.

Thank you to Hans Spoelman for your wonderfully creative designs.

Thank you to all my clients, friends and colleagues who have contributed to The Feminine Codes book, it would not exist if you hadn't requested and contributed to its contents.

Special thanks to Shambala Wegner, Naomi Chiffi, Charlotte Reynolds, Emma Sabin, Helena Holrick and Daisy Jane Veale for all your Personal Feminine Empowerment Journeys.

Thank you to my husband, Toby, for being my rock in life. You are such a generous, kind and supportive soul. I love you to the moon and back, and I am so lucky to have you as my best friend.

Thank you to my wonderful and inspirational daughters, Gem and KC. You are both the most amazing teachers a Mum could ever wish for. Authentic to the core. You are beautiful examples of how to live in a balance of both masculinity and femininity. I love you both.

Author Bio

Belinda grew up a vicar's daughter in the North of England. At fourteen and a punk, Belinda decided she wanted to get pregnant.

As a teenage Mum of two girls, Belinda struggled to keep her head above water financially, mentally and emotionally. She was a single parent on benefits in her early twenties, and she decided to take action. Belinda embraced her masculine side as the provider of everything for her small family of three. She took the brave decision to study Law full-time at University. Working part-time whilst studying to supplement a tiny student grant was tough, but she was determined to earn a decent salary to provide a good life for her children.

After graduating with a 2:1, Belinda quickly climbed up her chosen career ladder and personified her masculine traits. She had short dark hair, glasses, pinstripe trouser suits and flat shoes, a gym obsession and male friends. She was in no way feminine and totally disconnected from her feminine energy.

Twenty-plus years ago, that changed. Belinda left her career and husband in the same week and started on a journey to discover herself. She had carried her masculine shield for many years to protect herself from getting hurt. It had worked very well, but it had also blocked her feminine heart from being loved the way she really wanted, and it was time to rectify it. It took years of tough inner work to finally discover, understand, and embrace her femininity to live an authentic, whole, balanced life.

To find out more please read her inspirational memoir - Pregnant Punk at 14, Empowered at 50. Available on Amazon.

Belinda now lives in Ibiza with her husband and furry family in the countryside.

Belinda's two grown-up daughters are tremendous examples of empowered women with their own businesses and a perfect balance of masculine and feminine energies.

Belinda has been asked by many to write a book about the work she does with her clients. She's gathered all the lessons from her many years of personal experience and professional knowledge (Life Coach Dip, NLP Practitioner, Post Grad Certs in Coaching Psychology, Positive Psychology and Teaching) to craft The Feminine Codes for you, as well as her empowerment courses and programmes created with the intention of making your personal journey a whole lot easier.

Belinda desires to inspire everyone to nurture and value their feminine energy to enable a more harmonious and balanced world for all. She wishes millions of women worldwide wake up to the beauty of their unique femininity, embrace it and show it off for all the world to see. It is your divine right, truth and heritage.

CHAPTER 1

Introduction

"What do you mean you don't want to be supervised by me? I am your boss. That's my job, and I WILL supervise you!"

I was furious. These were the exact words I said to one of my team the week before my manager sacked me! I had sprinted to the top of my career ladder in criminal justice. I found myself far too much in my masculine energy, meaning I struggled in my new management position, forcing and pushing everything to enforce new changes and make it all work my way.

Up until this point, I had been very successful in managing people. And now one of my new team members was saying she didn't like how I managed employees and didn't want to be managed by me. I was livid and didn't know what to do, feeling like I had no tools to navigate such a situation. My anger made me feel I was lacking in control. I was at a loss, stressed and up shit creek without a paddle.

I know I'm not the only one to have felt like this. Have you ever found yourself in a similar situation? Without the tools to navigate and respond adequately? It doesn't need to be at work, it could be a personal relationship argument.

If so, this book can help you.

As the American Psychologist Abraham Maslow said, *"If you only have a hammer, you tend to see every problem as a nail."*

My intention with The Feminine Codes is to equip you with more tools so that you have a fuller toolbox and can choose the most appropriate tool for the job at hand.

Why it's essential to unlock your own Feminine Codes

For years the feminine has been suppressed, and as such, so many of us are living out of balance with a dominant inner masculine. Femininity is your divine right, truth and heritage - a dormant skill set within your sleepy DNA. It's time to reawaken these aspects to have a balanced set of masculine and feminine tools and techniques at your fingertips to select the right one for the situation at hand.

I've created the Feminine Codes to help women who feel like they have overdeveloped masculine traits or just want more tools and techniques to unlock their underdeveloped feminine traits, consciously utilise and balance both, and be the whole you, a unique blend of authentic masculine and feminine to live a happy, healthy, balanced life.

It's an easier, calmer and more authentic way to live as a woman in a society where we, as women, disempower ourselves and other women. A society where we have forgotten what it really means to be feminine and are unaware that women naturally operate differently from men.

The Feminine Codes is a step-by-step guide of bite-size chunks of awareness, action, and empowerment made easy. The tools and techniques within this book enabled me to understand how my mind and body work and to gain the best from my unique womanhood.

This book is here to help you navigate and discover what femininity is for you and how to use it to create more flow, harmony and balance, which can often seem very difficult in a world geared up to champion masculine traits as all that matters and is needed for a successful life. I'll introduce you to new skills and tools to unlock your natural feminine state to feel balanced, harmonious and at peace with yourself.

"We are judged by masculine criteria for success – and inevitably, we fall short because we are not men." Sharon Blackie

Let's get one thing straight: this is not a male-bashing book. The Feminine Codes is a way of life. A way to balance and harmonise both the masculine and feminine within.

Masculinity is embedded in everything we do, how we are taught to think, act, design, communicate, look, feel, and behave. Femininity is underrated and often seen as a weakness and inferior. As such, we often find ourselves overdeveloped in our masculine ways and severely lacking in our feminine ways. For example, my overdeveloped masculinity started at University while studying Law. As students, we were slowly but surely brainwashed and channelled into a masculine, logical, structured and intellectual way of thinking. During my first lecture, we were all told that we would never come up with anything that someone hadn't thought of and written about before, so don't bother to try. From that day on, my feminine side faded deep into the background, gradually getting quieter, quieter, and invisible from sight.

"If any human being is to reach full maturity, both the masculine and the feminine sides of the personality must be brought up into consciousness." Dr. Mary Esther Harding

The 7 Codes of Feminine Power

I know this is a big and complex topic, and there are many different approaches to femininity and gender; this is just one - my specific way and what worked for me.

Each chapter of The Feminine Codes links to the next and builds a stable and strong framework for exploring, developing, and creating your feminine power.

There are 7 Codes of Femininity to Discover:

Creativity

Compassion

Communication

Confidence

Care

Connection

Collaboration

The Feminine Codes acts as a guide and includes exercises to complete along your discovery journey and journaling prompts. I suggest you buy a notepad for these or buy my Feminine Codes Journal from Amazon, created especially to fit alongside this book. Journaling is an excellent tool for helping you to get your thoughts out of your head and down onto paper, as well as a brilliant way to help you connect to and express your feelings, making way for inner calm and clarity. It's one of the best ways I know to process any situation or issue.

As you work through this book, a world of potentiality will open up to you, expanding your very being. You'll find you're no longer struggling internally. Instead, everything slots into place from a space of ease and flow.

Are you ready to discover The Feminine Codes, unlock your unique femininity, and step into your true confidence and power?

PART 1:

Clarity

CHAPTER 2

Your Natural Feminine Characteristics

"The lioness does not try to be the lion. She embraces her role as the lioness. She is powerful, strong, and nurturing. She does not mistake her meekness for weakness. The world needs more kind, compassionate, humble, faithful, persevering, confident, fierce, bold, pure and tender-hearted women."

Lisa Bevere - Lioness Arising.

We can describe femininity as the natural characteristics of the human female species.

"Women weren't created to do everything a man can do. Women were created to do everything a man can't do." Unknown

We are not here to compete but to be in harmony. To learn how to balance our masculine and feminine sides for wholeness.

But whether we like it or not, we live in a patriarchal society where men predominantly hold most of the positions of power. A system where the qualities we identify as masculine are also the qualities of people in positions of power regardless of gender.

We find that the more women strive to prove they can and will do everything that a man can do, the more we are overdeveloping our masculinity and losing our unique and innate femininity - the very source of our power as women.

What exactly is this unique femininity?

It is your natural and innate characteristics as a female - caring, sharing, kind, compassionate, sensitive, intuitive, creative and open-hearted – these are just a few common female traits.

Traits, although we are born with and are inherent, often lay dormant or underutilised as we're encouraged to be proactive and not get emotional. Some of us still need to learn to see our feminine traits as strengths, not weaknesses. Asking for help must be one of the best examples I know. I used to hate asking for help, seeing it as a weakness rather than an opportunity to allow someone to feel good about themselves for helping me. Once I changed my mindset about asking for help, I realised I didn't get stressed as much, and people enjoyed helping me, creating a win-win.

Our patriarchal society has programmed us to value masculine or Yang qualities like dominance, assertion, projection and action instead of feminine Yin qualities like understanding, listening, vulnerability and collaboration. The good news is that there is room and a place for both within us all. My intention for you is to balance your overdeveloped masculine with your underdeveloped feminine. The transformation process to unlock your unique femininity starts from within, through awareness and connection to your unique femininity.

It's time to start to get curious about your feminine characteristics. Use exercise 1 to familiarise yourself with these natural traits. Identify which ones you resonate with and begin to integrate them into your life.

Exercise 1 - List of Feminine Characteristics

Friendly	**Creative**
Affectionate	**Nurturing**
Kind	**Loving**
Expressive	**Gentle**
Graceful	**Tender**
Inclusive	**Compassionate**
Supportive	**Sensitive**
Helpful	**Tactful**
Forgiving	**Emotional**
Patient	**Caring**
Empathetic	**Considerate**

Tick those that resonate with you, and then write an intention for your unique femininity in your journal.

An intention is a sentence or two about something you want to happen. For example, my intention for my unique femininity is to be more inclusive and supportive of others and more nurturing to myself.

Cycles of the Feminine

"Most women are taught from an early age that our period, and really our entire menstrual cycle, is a pain in the ass. It's a nuisance we have to put up with, an event filled with shame, pain, and embarrassment. In that, we are taught how to reject a key aspect of our bodies as well as the biological mechanism that gives rise to life. We tend not to honour ourselves and the hormonal fluctuations that occur naturally in our bodies, and so we remain detached from how to tune into our own inner wisdom." Caroline Zwickson

This is staggeringly true. Many young girls grow up not knowing about key aspects of being a female, myself included. The only information I received about puberty was a pamphlet written by nuns and left on my bed when I was eleven. I was terrified when my first period arrived. Not feeling comfortable telling my Mum, I made my own sanitary pads from cotton wool and toilet roll for the first few months. As adult women, we reject our natural cycles month after month. If we don't know why we behave the way we do, what hope do men have of understanding what's happening?

The feminine cycle isn't just about menstruation and periods. It also incorporates our hormone cycles and affects us whether we are bleeding or not. Our responsibility as a woman is to educate ourselves, our partners, employers and children about what's going on and why.

I come from a school of thought whereby women and men are inherently different. Yes, we are part of the same species, but we have distinctive physical and mental differences. For example, women are cyclical by nature and are connected to the rhythms of nature and the moon's cycles. The full moon is a time of creation and productivity; you may be full of energy and find sleeping difficult. The new moon is a time of resting and retreating; you may feel tired and lacking energy. Women follow the moon cycle.

Our lives initially revolve around our menstruation cycle, which is connected to the lunar cycle and influences our hormones and state of being (whether we are bleeding or not). Within this monthly cycle, we are a different woman each week. As Caroline Zwickson explains, our energies shift as we move through the weekly cycles of:

Winter (the week of your period: sensitive, low on energy, needs more rest).

Spring (the week after your period: energised, productive and happy).

Summer (mid cycle: creative, social and nurturing).

Autumn/Fall (the week before your period: moody, assertive and tired).

Awareness of this cycle helped me identify and understand why I might be experiencing different reactions at different times of the month, such as feeling tired and moody or full of beans and happy. This cycle has continued, to a lesser degree, even after menopause.

By contrast, men and the masculine are lineal and hold a linear view of time and events. Men naturally follow the sun.

Society is patriarchal and linear-led, making it difficult to acknowledge and understand our differences as females. But once we are aware and paying attention, it makes it much easier to live together more harmoniously, complementing each other as the yin and yang of life. The struggle occurs when a woman tries to operate like a man from a linear perspective, skewing the natural order of her life. She may achieve a lot, but not in an authentic, heart-centred way aligned with the feminine. Deep down, she will not be truly happy or fulfilled under the layers of acting that have become the norm. Taking on a male persona and embodying masculine traits goes against her natural way of being. Long-term, this can cause emotional pain and potentially physical illness.

I have first-hand experience of this. In my twenties, I adopted a male persona to get on professionally and advance the career ladder. I decided it would help me in my work life if I became more masculine, tough and competitive. I wore pinstripe trouser suits, flat shoes, short dark hair and glasses. I was bossy, aggressive and unemotional - something I couldn't sustain. At age thirty-three, everything changed. After three months, I was sacked from my new position at work and sent back to my old job. I didn't even last a day in my old job again before I quit. I realised I was unhappy and unbalanced, and something had to shift.

I consciously decided to take time out from my all-consuming career, as I was suffering from burnout and symptoms of being overwhelmed. I stopped my life and took a six-month life sabbatical. By giving myself space and slowing down, learning to align with my feminine rhythms and traits began to draw me. I took long walks in nature and questioned what I wanted to do with my life. I did a life audit while my career was on hold for six months. I asked myself questions like: what did I really want from life? What made me happy, and what didn't? What needed to change, and how would I make that happen?

It was a brave step that totally transformed my whole life. I devised a six-month plan that included leaving my husband, learning to windsurf and changing my career! As I was still so much in my masculinity, I logically thought six months was plenty of time to achieve all this.

My mother thought I was having a breakdown and offered to look after the children whilst I went off to be a waitress in Italy or somewhere exotic. I reassured her that I hadn't felt this clear, good or free in a very, very long time. I had no desire whatsoever to be a waitress in Italy (no offence to all you waitresses in Italy, but it's just not my thing).

Three signs you're disconnected from your feminine power:

1. You continue to try to force things to happen.
2. You ignore your monthly cycle and carry on regardless.
3. You love to compete all the time with everyone.

If any of the above rings true for you, don't worry; this is normal when living in overdeveloped masculinity. Be kind to yourself and start to become aware.

Exercise 2 - Cycles of the Feminine

Now you have been introduced to the natural cycles of the feminine –

Winter

Spring

Summer

Autumn/Fall

Please familiarise yourself a little more with your cycles and how your feminine body changes weekly. Even if you are not bleeding, your body is still going through female automatic and hormonal cycles.

Do your own research online on the Cycles of the Feminine. By learning more about yourself, you will be in a better position to understand your reactions and behaviour and be able to explain them to others, too.

Identify and write down in your journal where you are in your cycle now and how you are feeling. This is helpful even if you are not bleeding.

The Feminine Mindset

We have looked at some of the major differences between masculine and feminine natural characteristics. It is also important to be aware of the difference in mindsets. A mindset is a person's mental state or attitude, innately different depending on individual circumstances, gender and environment.

The male mindset focuses traditionally on dominance, leadership, charm, confidence and focus.

"Women, its known, retain stronger, more vivid memories of emotional events than men do. They recall emotional memories more quickly, and the ones they recall are richer and more intense. Men, on average, can more easily juggle items in working memory. They have superior visuospatial skills: They're better at visualising what happens when a complicated two or three-dimensional shape is rotated in space." Bruce Goldman

The bestselling book Men Are From Mars, Women Are From Venus by John Gray helped to establish how men and women are different in thought and behaviour. The book's basic premise is that relationships between men and women can improve if their differences in needs, desires and behaviours are acknowledged. More often than not, society has programmed us to think from a male mindset, as that is our society's way. This often takes the form of: 'Stop being so emotional; just get on with it and find a solution!'

But there is another, better way. We, as women, have the choice to learn to work with our feminine mindset. When we operate this way, we feel better about ourselves and more connected to who we are. More confident, balanced and at peace.

How do we do this?

One of the best ways I know and often use to connect to my feminine side is by spending time in nature alone, either walking amongst trees, through fields or in a park or by sitting quietly surrounded by shrubs, trees, grass and the odd bird.

Another great way to connect to your feminine is to make time to be present, listen, observe and assess. To create awareness, ask questions and learn patience. Connecting to our feminine traits and adopting a feminine mindset with thinking habits aligned with our natural state allows us to open up to the potentiality that lies deep within.

According to Megan Dalla-Camina and Michelle McQuaid, it's all about *"allowing women to show up and use their feminine traits like compassion, collaboration, empathy, vulnerability, and intuition and see them for what they are – natural strengths – and value them in workplaces."*

It's not about how well a woman can adapt to a masculine lead environment. It's about asking questions to include and respect feminine traits as essential qualities to complement masculinity - traits like patience, inclusivity, guidance and compassion.

Megan goes on to say, *"Perhaps the question is how do we as women, as individuals and as a collective, become so empowered and clear and conscious and connected that workplaces have no choice but to evolve into an entirely new system that must elevate to meet the new consciousness that women create in the world."*

In developing a feminine mindset, we must also learn how to receive. This is unfamiliar territory to many people and, in my experience, especially women. Many women are used to giving their time and energy to others; as wives, partners, mothers, daughters, sisters, etc., we give, give, give. Receiving can seem like an alien concept, one that takes practice. It can feel strange and uncomfortable initially, but try not to deny others giving to you. Just like you like to give, allow others to give to you also.

Try the following exercise and create positive change affirmations.

Exercise 3 - My Unique Feminine Affirmations

By taking the feminine characteristics that resonated with you from exercise one, you can now start to make space, allow them to manifest in your life, and embody them as second nature.

Using the words from exercise one and other words that describe feminine characteristics that resonate with you, create and write down below or in your journal three unique feminine affirmations just for you to repeat every day until they feel like part of you and automatic.

An affirmation is a specific, positive statement personal to you and written in the present tense, for example -

- I am a supportive and loving friend.
- I enjoy practising my nurturing ways every day.

Write your affirmations in your journal and read them daily.

PART 2:

The 7 Feminine Codes

CHAPTER 3

Code 1 - Creativity

"Creativity is not a talent; it's a way of operating."

John Cleese

These are the words John Cleese declared in his lecture on creativity, as featured in his Genius.com article. John says creativity can't be explained and likens it to being open instead of being closed when you're at work and tense.

So, I'm going to attempt to explain the unexplainable. Contrary to popular opinion or what I call, patriarchal masking, where logic is respected far more than creativity, the term creativity is not all about painting, writing, drawing and crocheting. Creativity is also about dreaming up ideas, problem-solving, connecting thoughts and being in this world.

Creativity is an innate feminine trait within us all, regardless of gender. Creative instinct is accessible to anyone who wants to utilise it. Yet, we live in a world that puts logic before creativity (patriarchal masking). We struggle daily to manipulate life and force situations to happen instead of allowing things to flow at their own pace. This indicates the patriarchal working environment, the closed one that John refers to above. Therefore, it's unsurprising that creativity is not a widely respected and utilised tool when trying to live your best life.

Creativity is a biological basic function: from seeds into trees, spiders weaving intricate webs, babies being born to all species and food growing from our earth. Creativity in nature is everywhere, yet how often do you notice and acknowledge it? Most people are too busy, hurrying from one appointment to the other, unconscious of the creative energy that surrounds us and is available to us daily.

"Creativity is the counterbalance to logic and rigid systems. It's what makes us feel alive and inspired to live life." Belinda M Clarke.

Without creativity, we wouldn't have mobile phones, wifi, electric cars, computers and the implement you're reading this from. These are everyday tools that we often take for granted. Creativity is the basis of all ideas and solutions and the basis of all life. Creativity is openness. Creativity needs to be felt and nurtured in your heart, not just your head. To do this you must connect your heart and head to access your creativity. This takes practise as most of us live in our heads, detached energetically from our bodies.

How are you honouring your creativity?

Do you know how to nurture and grow those ideas that flow from your head?

How do you know if you are using your creative instinct? Here's an exercise to find out:

Exercise 4 - Are You Creative?

Take a moment to reflect on what creativity means to you. Write in your journal the answers to these questions...

Do you consider yourself creative or not, and why?

How did it make you feel if you have ever been told that you're not creative?

What challenges are you experiencing about writing about creativity?

How has creativity benefitted you in the past?

What lessons and wisdom can you share about creativity?

AFFIRMATION

I am Creative

CHAPTER 4

Conscious Creativity

We've all experienced the feeling of being totally immersed in something we're doing, an activity that interests us. It could be a gripping conversation, cooking, reading, gardening, or anything.

This state is what Mihaly Csikszentmihalyi, the author of Flow: The Psychology of Optimal Experience, calls the 'flow state'. I studied his work whilst reading Positive Psychology at the University of East London. He defined flow as *'an optimal state of consciousness where we feel our best and perform our best'.*

Mihaly was a creativity researcher and interestingly linked flow to creativity. When we enter this state, all self-consciousness is lost. The self-consciousness part is key here. People tend to be self-conscious and hold themselves back from participating in an act for fear of appearing foolish or looking ridiculous. The flow state allows us to lose our self-consciousness and enter a fully creative form.

The answer to being creative must be to practise entering a flow state. How do you do that?

You must fully engage your head and heart to be consciously creative. Lucy H. Pearce is the author of a brilliant book called Creatrix. She has written extensively on the subject of creativity and states, *"When we create, we tend to feel more fully alive and fully aligned with the natural flow of the Universe than at any other time in our lives. It is what we were made for, what we are here to do".*

Patriarchy forces us to disown essential parts of us to gain power and control. Patriarchy blocks creativity. It knows how powerful creativity can be and uses psychology to insist it's for children, not important or needed.

As Lucy says, *'Creativity is in our veins; it's what we were made to do, to create.'* Creativity is our life force, meaning we can feel flat and empty without it.

If Lucy's words inspire you to incorporate more creativity into your life, how can you implement that? How can you weave more creativity into your life consciously?

Please take a moment to reflect on how you can be more creative in your life and write your answers in your journal.

Naturally wired to create

My top strength, as confirmed by the Via Institute on Character, is Creativity.

Naturally, I am a highly creative person who has always been that way inclined and will always be. I started baking cakes and biscuits on my own when I was nine, making my clothes at twelve, and creating a baby at fourteen. I upcycled lots of furniture while studying Law at University as a single-parent student. You get the picture; I'm creative. My creativity made me very resourceful as a young parent. I didn't have much money and had to get by on very little whilst feeding myself and two children.

Not everyone will have creativity as a top strength, but rest assured, as long as you're human, you are creative. The fun lies in finding out what creative things you like doing. Is it something with your hands like DIY, gardening or cooking? Or maybe it has more to do with your ideas, like helping a friend with their finances to afford a holiday or finding a cheaper utility provider. Reflect on when you were a child. What excited you most? Our life path comes from what we enjoyed most as a child. What made us most happy before society conditioned us into academic systems and employment is usually what makes our hearts leap as an adult. For example, my friend dreamed of being an author and writer as a child but got caught up in a corporate career once she'd left university. A few years ago, she broke free from the rat race, wrote her own book, and now happily helps others do the same while feeling fulfilled and useful.

What did you enjoy doing? Was it building, drawing, or making shapes out of the clouds?

I enjoyed being in nature, messing about in the garden and making dens under the bushes.

You don't have to have creativity as a top strength to be creative. The great thing is we all have creativity within our DNA. Your task is to unearth and be aware of it in your way, not mine. The opportunity of conscious creativity is to weave your own creations in whatever way speaks to you.

My creativity strength has come in extremely useful at work, too. Years ago, when a charity employed me, I had to create a welcoming and relaxed environment for young offenders to learn in. The budget was minimal, but with much imagination and creativity, my team and I created a fun and cosy place that the teenagers liked visiting.

Although my creativity can be helpful, it can be challenging, too. I often have a constant stream of ideas that need to be birthed but go nowhere. I write mine down and keep them safe on my desk if I want to refer back to them. For example, when we moved to Ibiza, my husband Toby and I sat down and made a list of every possible business we could start that didn't already exist – a Speciality Coffee Roastery, a Microbrewery, and a Water Bottling Plant, to name a few. We didn't follow through on them, although they all materialised over the years via other people. I like to think we're all connected to a conscious collective and just plugging in with others to a huge pool of ideas, but that's for another book.

I always come up with creative ideas for new businesses, not just for me but often in conversation with others. It's probably quite annoying, but I find it fun. I'm one of those people who think of a brilliant business idea, buy the domain and do nothing. I must have purchased hundreds of domains over the years!

I also like hands-on creativity, like cooking and painting. I can create a meal from scratch with the existing contents of my kitchen, without a recipe, in no time and enjoy the process, too. I love decorating and painting pictures, but not the preparation or fine detail. And that's okay with me. I'm not a perfectionist, as I'd rather have variety than spend time after time on the same thing. And that's okay with me, too. I often employ an expert coach to help me finish a work project. If you're the same, you may want to seek help from a business coach to get a project over the line.

I also feel at my most creative when I'm in nature. Connecting to the incredible and outstanding beauty of the outdoors is enough to fill me up, open my heart and inspire me with ideas. I utilise my senses, smelling the fresh air; currently, it's warm and piney as summer is coming. There can be scents of pine, fig, rosemary or carob, depending on the time of year. I can sit for ages listening to the birds sing, watching the ants take bits of twigs and seeds from one location to another, and noticing the plants growing and the flowers blooming. It calms my soul and regulates my inner being. I feel grounded and at peace whilst sitting in nature with my bare feet on the ground.

Trees are one of my favourite inspirations - strong and rooted, firm and bold, yet swaying gently in the breeze and providing a whole host of goodies for many different species of life - ants, spiders, birds and other creatures. We are blessed in Ibiza to have beautiful old trees everywhere. My favourites are the Holm Oak, an indigenous but now rare and protected variety. The Mediterranean Olive is gnarly, twisted and many thousands of years old, and the Umbrella Pine is tall and majestic and produces the delicious delicacy of pine nuts. I find trees incredibly powerful, and the most wondrous I've seen are in California, America. The Giant Redwoods and the Sequoia's towering above seventy metres high, or the equivalent of a twenty-five floor building, are incredible.

A friend of mine feels creative when she's by the sea – with the glistening water, patterns, sand shapes, seashells and seaweed. It all fills her heart with inspiration. She can spend ages sitting by the sea, developing new ideas and making notes.

Although creativity is a natural part of us all, due to our prior conditioning of patriarchal dominance, our creativity muscles are often weak and wobbly. Like any weak muscle, it needs use and exercise to become stronger and more effective. With awareness and practise, anyone can build their creativity, and you don't need to live in the countryside to do it. The intention is more important than the environment. Nature is everywhere: in a window box, garden, the local park, and even indoor potted plants.

CHAPTER 5

The Code to Creativity

Hopefully, this section has conveyed the importance of including creativity in your life to feel balanced and alive and inspired you to create more._You can cultivate creativity by open thinking, learning and exposing yourself to continued new experiences. Your brain is wired for creativity; utilise it.

Exercise 5 - How can you include more creativity in your life?

Try these:

- Make time and space to be more creative. Do what brings you joy.
- Balance out logic and systems work with expressive and creative flow.
- Buy a colouring book for adults and pens.
- Plant some seeds of herbs, flowers or tomatoes and tend to them.
- Cook from scratch with or without a recipe.

- Spend time alone self-reflecting.
- Join a writing group online.
- Make a bookmark from a pressed flower.
- Start a creative ideas scrapbook.

Play or listen to inspiring music.

Create a creative corner in your home. It could be a table in the corner of a room where you gather and store all your innovative materials to paint, draw, colour in, cut, stick, sew, and collect - a homage to your inner creative part.

Personal Feminine Empowerment Journey - Creativity

I'm not conventionally creative. I do not express my creativity by painting on a canvas or through notes plucked on a guitar. I do not do it through my body or hands, in dance, clay, or sculpture. I love and appreciate all these ways of expressing creativity, but I'm not particularly 'good' at them. I am a decent enough writer, but I think that might be a by-product of how my brand of creativity works.

I have been a trainer all my life (at four, I was teaching the other kids in the sand pit how to make castles "properly" or calming and encouraging them when their frustrations meant tears and too much noise – for me, anyway!). I'm a stitcher of information; intuition is my thread, instinct is my needle, and interest is my canvas. I've used this natural ability (aka creativity) to make ideas emerge, come alive, and land for years.

I'm creative this way: I innately see how things, abstract concepts and disparate thoughts link together. I am a connector of ideas. I am adept at seeing what's needed, what's missing and what can make things better. My creativity manifests in my drawing out of people what's in them; as a coach, guide and mentor, I somehow see what they can't. I hold space for people to see themselves differently. I can connect and hold all the seemingly unrelated parts, explain it patiently enough so it's understood, and then encourage people to do something with it.

I'm eternally curious, and I have learned to ask really good questions that move people from frustration to feeling great, fully functioning, and fascinated with life again. My creativity helps people get unstuck and out of being overwhelmed and find their way back to what makes them happy by connecting to their lives and creatively expressing themselves differently. That opens up opportunities, possibilities, and how my 'magic' (aka creativity) works. My wish for the world is that every person learns to understand, respect, express and use their unique gifts, i.e., creativity.

A long time ago, I connected the dots of what I love, what I'm good at, what matters to me and what people seem to appreciate about what I do for them. I took all those things and turned them into my work. You could say that's my ultimate creation.

Helena Holrick - Chief Cheerleader, Helping You Shine.

CHAPTER 6

Code 2 – Compassion

In my experience as a therapist and coach, compassion is a word often misused. Knowing which word to use can be confusing, depending on the situation. Many people get compassion confused with sympathy and empathy, and differences exist.

I used to get them all confused. I would often think I was being compassionate, but actually, I was being sympathetic. I remember doing research into compassion and having a conversation about it with my Dad. I asked him if he thought he was compassionate.

He replied, "I'm very sympathetic", and walked off.

I was in my thirties when I discovered the true meaning of compassion. Until then, I assumed, like most people, that I knew what compassion was. I was very wrong. It took a heated disagreement with a friend twenty years ago to realise that maybe I didn't know the real meaning of compassion, and especially in my line of work, it was time that I found out. So that is exactly what I did.

The Merriam-Webster dictionary defines compassion as *"sympathetic consciousness of others' distress, together with a desire to alleviate it"*.

Sympathy or concern for others, is only an element of compassion. The desire to do something about others' distress turns sympathy into compassion. Yet most people stop at sympathy.

The meaning of empathy can also be confusing, here's the official line...

'Empathy refers to an active sharing in the emotional experience of the other person.' Merriam-Webster Dictionary

Compassion, at its simplest, is about having concern and sharing the emotional experience of another **and** the desire to do something about it. Compassion has evolved over the past few decades, and I strongly feel that it is important for everyone to learn its true meaning and power.

To have compassion, you need to notice that the other is suffering, be moved by their pain, which may be emotional, mental or physical, and want to do something about it.

Brene Brown has written extensively on Compassion and has this to say *"Compassion is not a virtue – it is a commitment. It's not something we have or don't have – it's something we choose to practice."*

I agree that compassion is something you practise and the more you practise the better you are at it. I'm happy that I discovered the true meaning of compassion, turned it into a superpower and used it as the antidote to criticism. I can't stress enough how well it works, not only for myself but for many, many clients, too.

Katie had been having a tough time at work with her colleagues, feeling excluded and sidelined. By introducing the concept of compassion to Katie, she started to see that she was the one who was shunning her work colleagues by not joining in their conversations. As such, they'd stopped trying to include her.

Compassion allows you to see a whole new perspective on a situation, like discovering a new room in your house. Compassion is the gift that keeps on giving. Once understood and practised, you get to enjoy a sense of inner calm by moving away from separatism and towards a connection to everyone and everything.

According to Chris Irons and Elaine Beaumont in their book The Compassionate Mind Workbook, there are three core qualities of compassion: Wisdom, Caring-commitment, Strength and courage. Here is my understanding...

1. Wisdom

Wisdom is an integral quality to be able to act compassionately. For example, if on a plane and the oxygen masks drop to be used, ensure you put your own mask on first before helping others with theirs. If you don't, you may be unable to help anyone else as you may be unconscious.

2. Caring-commitment

Compassion is a warm, feminine quality, hence the need for a kind and caring approach. Being compassionate is based on using emotional experience and taking responsibility to act. You cannot be compassionate without being emotional and engaged in another's suffering.

3. Strength and courage

To be truly compassionate takes a lot of strength and courage. To involve yourself in your own or another's distress takes guts. Combined with wisdom and caring commitment, strength and courage are essential ingredients to perfect the mix for effective compassion.

Compassion will inevitably flourish by reflecting on each of the above and developing all three.

Exercise 6 - The Roots of Compassion

Sit quietly and upright, somewhere that you won't be disturbed. Close your eyes. Breathe in and out slowly three times, then breathe normally for you.

Now imagine you have roots growing from the bottom of your feet down into the earth, just like a tree. You notice that you have three large roots growing in different directions but very much connected to the same tree. These three roots are Wisdom, Care and Strength. Focus on these three main roots for a few minutes, noticing what they look like and reflecting on examples of where in your life you show up as Wise, Caring and Strong.

When you've finished and are ready, take three deep breaths, feel your feet firmly on the ground, stretch and gently open your eyes.

Write down your experience in your journal.

AFFIRMATION

I am Compassion

CHAPTER 7

Why Compassion Is Your Superpower

I stated earlier that compassion is my superpower, but it's not just me that can benefit. Everyone can develop compassion and use it as a superpower if only they knew about it. I didn't once upon a time. It is your biggest secret tool to empowerment and authentic confidence.

As Paul Gilbert OBE, states: *"Compassion isn't just this nice feeling; it's the preparedness to turn towards difficulty... to be sensitive to suffering for yourself and others."*

When appropriately used, compassion is a very powerful tool. As we saw in the last section, it takes guts, real strength and courage, combined with emotional care and the understanding and experience to act correctly and put all that into practice. It's not a simple task. Now, you can see how people can easily misunderstand compassion. It is a complex action that entails many parts and much responsibility.

Practising compassion is a new way for many of us and how we view the world. It's a practice that can help you, as a woman, respond in a calmer and more understanding manner with more space. It is a way that can help society as a whole – because the more compassionate people are, the less time and energy get wasted, and the less narcissistic people become. This is why I view compassion as a superpower.

While studying for my postgraduate qualification in Psychology, I spent much time researching compassion and how it feels in your body. Your heart rate slows down, the empathic centres of your brain light up, producing feelings of caregiving, and we flood every cell with extra oxytocin, the bonding hormone, to make you feel good about what you're doing.

"Yesterday, I was clever, so I wanted to change the world. Today I am wise, so I am changing myself." Rumi

Compassion can change lives for the better. We have no idea what's going on in another's life. So why not be compassionate and trust that they have a good reason to do what they do? That reason could stem from anything from fear to life programming.

Being compassionate involves more than feeling sorry for someone, wanting to help or putting yourself in their shoes. It involves an emotional connection with the experience, creating a new perspective and acting effectively. Compassion is important for women, as it's vital for increasing self-esteem and leading a happy and more fulfilled life. More women tend to have low self-esteem than men.

"Men generally have higher self-esteem and subjective well-being than women" Ruth Derdikman-Eiron

Compassion is a feminine trait that helps everyone when utilised more often. Yes it requires a little vulnerability and humility but it's totally worth it.

"Humans have evolved to need love, affection and compassion to varying degrees throughout life." Paul Gilbert

How do you practise compassion? Please see the exercise below.

Exercise 7 - Practising Compassion:

Now you are familiar with what compassion truly is, please demonstrate how you practise your new superpower by doing one intentional act of compassion for another over the next few days.

Write your findings down in your journal and answer the following:

- What was the compassionate act you did?
- How did the recipient respond?
- How did you feel? Identify your emotions, e.g. vulnerable, anxious, happy etc.

CHAPTER 8

The Antidote to Self-Judgement is Self-Compassion

Having compassion for yourself is as important as having compassion for others. One can describe self-compassion as being kind, gentle, aware and understanding towards yourself instead of criticising and judging yourself harshly. It is about caring for yourself and honouring your human failings.

Doing this involves noticing when you need to be comforted and looked after. Instead of ignoring it or telling yourself to 'pull your socks up', treat yourself like you would a good friend. You wouldn't talk to your friend with a harsh, negative tone, so why do it to yourself?

Being compassionate towards yourself has many benefits. Research shows that you're more likely to have higher self-esteem and be less self-critical if you're self-compassionate. You are also more likely to have less anxiety and depression and be happier, more optimistic and more positive.

As Dr. Kristin Neff, a pioneer of self-compassion, states: *"Self-compassion is a powerful way to achieve emotional well-being and contentment in our lives, helping us avoid destructive patterns of fear, negativity, and isolation."*

Self-compassion is a power source. If compassion is a superpower, self-compassion is a superpower on steroids! Self-compassion is a way to connect to yourself and get out of your head and into your body more. It helps to bring you awareness of your feelings and what those feelings are trying to tell you. Self-compassion works especially well regarding emotions, helping us recognise life's difficulties as inevitable and providing us with a powerful and effective tool for choosing a calm, thoughtful and helpful response. Open your heart and give yourself this gift.

Please see the exercise below to take the free Self-Compassion Test and learn more about this practice.

Exercise 8 - Self-Compassion Test

Now that you are familiar with what self-compassion is and how it can benefit you, please follow the link below to The Center For Mindful Self Compassion (centerformsc.org) and complete the test; it's free and only takes a few moments.

https://centerformsc.org/learn-msc/take-the-self-compassion-test/

Write down your test results in your journal.
If you would like to raise your self-compassion, write a positive and loving letter to yourself thanking yourself for being alive and aware.

The Power of Forgiveness

The more you practise self-compassion, the more you can open up to the concept of forgiveness of self and others. Understanding and utilising forgiveness is critical in releasing stored toxic negativity that causes stress, deep sadness, and disease. This leads to greater self-belief, gratitude for life and self-confidence.

"Forgiveness liberates the soul; it removes fear. That's why it's such a powerful weapon." Nelson Mandela

Nelson was imprisoned for twenty-seven years and suffered severe beatings for objecting to apartheid. On his release, he called for forgiveness.

Psychologists generally define forgiveness as a conscious, deliberate decision to release feelings of resentment or vengeance toward a person or group who has harmed you, regardless of whether they actually deserve your forgiveness.

This powerful weapon that Nelson Mandela talks of is most potent for you, the forgiver.To forgive is not to condone wrong actions or ignore a serious offence. Instead, it releases the one doing the forgiving from the consequences of negative emotions like hatred and anger. These toxic emotions can eat away at our very centre and have the power to create physical disease and illness. Forgiveness allows us to make way for healing and empowerment.

One of my favourite forgiveness quotes that I find really powerful is from Lewis B. Smedes, who wrote a lot about the power of forgiveness - *"To forgive is to set a prisoner free and discover that the prisoner was you."*

While working on my self-development, I discovered that the only person I was hurting by not forgiving those in my life that I perceived to have done me wrong was me! Like everyone, I had people in my life that I held a grudge against. People that had hurt me physically and emotionally. I was very angry and upset until I realised I was hurting myself more by holding onto and imprisoning myself. Realising that I was the one with the key to my prison door and could set myself free anytime was transformative.

The practice of compassion is the gateway to forgiveness. Master the habit of compassion to smooth the way for yourself, and you will find it much easier when the need for forgiveness arises – and trust me, it will.

To sum up, forgiveness isn't for the other's benefit; it's for our own. Forgiveness frees you from self-imposed shackles and propels you into a place of healing and transformation.

The following exercise will help you to free yourself through the power of forgiveness.

Exercise 9 - The Power of Forgiveness

Please take a few minutes to think about the people in your life that you have a grudge against. These people may have hurt you emotionally or physically.

Then, make a list in your journal of the names of these people in your life who have done you wrong in some way and whom you haven't forgiven yet. Be honest, as sometimes we think we've forgiven people. However, when you think about them, and you're still angry with them, this means that you haven't truly forgiven them.

Using what you have learned about your superpower of compassion and the benefits of forgiveness, forgive the people on the list and free yourself from that negative, destructive hold.

Personal Feminine Empowerment Journey - Compassion

Being diagnosed with late-stage breast cancer at age forty was one of the most traumatic and challenging things to happen to my life, challenging me physically, emotionally, and mentally. I was left grappling with uncertainty and fear.

There were days when the weight of my diagnosis felt unbearable, and I struggled to maintain a positive outlook. I was meant to be the prime of my life, yet I'd had to have a double mastectomy and lost the chance to be a natural mum. I felt alone, and some days I questioned my future.

During my recovery, the journey tested my physical strength. It also pushed me to explore the depths of my emotional and spiritual selves. As I confronted this life-altering diagnosis, I discovered a powerful source of healing within by embracing my feminine side, the yin energy that my more dominant masculine yang energy had long overshadowed.

For years, I'd lived a life driven by the ideals of strength, assertiveness, and control. I was a sales director at a London publishing house, so these more yang traits were useful for my career but were not attributes for healing my mind, body or soul. The one key tool that proved invaluable in my return to health was learning to find self-compassion, an unexpected source of empowerment. I had to show myself the compassion I had previously reserved for others. It was not a coincidence that the two tumours had been in my left breast; studies regard this as the feminine side of the body, the receiving side - where you take in love. As the eldest in a family where I had taken on the caring role and the head of a sales team where the company paid me to take charge, giving instead of receiving was what I was accustomed to.

I allowed myself to feel the fear, pain and uncertainty of battling a life-threatening illness. Instead of trying to control every aspect of my treatment and prognosis, I surrendered to the process. I embraced the receptive and nurturing qualities of yin energy. I started to practise mindfulness and meditation, techniques that enabled me to connect with my body on a profound level. I learned to listen to its whispers, to feel the rhythm of its healing, and to honour the signals it sent me. Through these practices, I began to appreciate the intricate wisdom of my body, realising that healing wasn't just about eradicating the cancerous cells but also about restoring harmony within myself.

As I embraced my feminine side, I engaged in creative outlets that had always intrigued me. I returned to my old activities of dancing, singing and exploring nature with a renewed sense of wonder. These activities allowed me to express my emotions freely and unapologetically, transcending the limitations of words. Through this creative process, I uncovered layers of myself I had buried beneath the demands of a yang-dominated lifestyle. I realised I had to follow my lifelong dream – to dance and work with children – which led me to study Dance Movement Psychotherapy and Children's Yoga Teacher Training. Ten years on, now living in Ibiza, I wholeheartedly believe that all my training has played a big part in my recovery.

What surprised me most was how connecting with my yin energy didn't just support my physical healing but also fostered a profound sense of wholeness and self-acceptance. I began to view my cancer journey as an opportunity for transformation rather than a mere obstacle to overcome. This perspective shift allowed me to release the need to prove my strength to the world and instead focus on nurturing my inner world.

Opening up to my feminine side wasn't about rejecting my yang energy but finding balance and integration. I realised that true healing came from embracing both aspects of myself, allowing them to complement and support one another. My treatments became more effective, and my overall outlook on life became more positive.

Ultimately, my journey through breast cancer became a testament to the transformative power of embracing one's whole self.

Emma Sabin - Shine Through Cancer Coach

CHAPTER 9

Code 3 - Communication

Even if we speak the same language and are conversing about the same topic, misunderstandings between people are very common. This is especially true in our age of technology. Tech can connect us very easily to others in different parts of the world. Still, miscommunication happens all the time as we don't pick up on nuances like tone of voice, body language, facial expressions, etc. That's where the need for effective communication comes in.

Effective communication is more than just exchanging information. Entwined with the words we speak are non-verbal communications from our tone to emotions, intentions and body language. However, most of us don't fully listen to what others say. We're often too busy thinking about what we should say next. We have all witnessed this during a conversation. Sometimes, it's ourselves thinking about what we will say next, and sometimes the other person. But often, it's all parties of the conversation, making it seem more like a take-your-turn game than a conscious flowing conversation.

I used to be terrible at actively participating fully in a conversation. I would spend the time when I wasn't speaking thinking of great things to say in 'response' whilst the other was talking, not having listened to what they were actually saying. I was far too interested in getting my points across. That was until I discovered and learnt active listening during my counselling training. It transformed my conversations from a verbal ping-pong match to a flowing, enjoyable stream of engaged conversation.

Practising Active Listening, a technique developed by Carl Rogers, can help you take in what others say verbally and non-verbally.

"It is called active because the listener has a definite responsibility. He does not passively absorb the words which are spoken to him. He actively tries to grasp the facts and feelings in what he hears." Carl R. Rogers and Richard Evans Farson

Active listening is first-level engaged listening, requiring the listener to give their full attention to what others say. Then there is Empathic Listening. This requires active, engaged listening and the use of empathy too. Here, the listener will also focus on understanding the speaker's emotional experience.

Empathic listening is very useful when understanding what the other person is saying. It ensures the listener focuses deeply, giving the speaker extra confidence that the listener understood. This is used a lot in therapy but isn't exclusive and can be a beneficial and worthwhile skill to learn.

Active and Empathic Listening are not automatic skills. We have to learn how to fully hear another person and understand the meaning of what others communicate. Just like we learn to read and write as a child, learning how to listen fully would be useful, but listening somehow gets forgotten. It's never too late to learn how to listen at an engaged level, although you do need the desire to do so.

We also need to learn how to convey our own messages clearly. It takes time, practise, vulnerability and, again, the desire to do so. We often feel embarrassed or shy at expressing our opinions or speaking to people we don't know. It's very common to have an uncomfortable feeling as conversation is a skill many haven't practised growing up; it takes courage to put yourself out there.

Victoria, a client, was raised to be a quiet, good girl by her parents. This meant keeping herself to herself, not interrupting any grown-up conversations and remaining silent in public. Unfortunately, this kind of training from a very young age until adulthood created very limited beliefs for Victoria. She believed herself not worthy of any opinions and that no one ever wanted to hear anything she had to say.

Victoria avoided public events that may mean she'd have to speak to strangers or people she didn't really know. She felt anxious if anyone asked her opinion at work and spent a lot of time trying to be invisible. Victoria initially found it incredibly difficult to have a conversation with me. Still, on a one-to-one level, she soon opened up and started to look forward to her therapy sessions. Gradually, Victoria learnt how to have a flowing conversation and quickly realised she had excellent listening skills and a very good line of genuine inquisitive questions. Victoria started to find conversations interesting, as if she was making up for lost time.

Like Victoria, the results are absolutely transformative if you practise and learn good communication skills. It's like learning a new language - a gateway to another world. Good communication helps to minimise misunderstandings and reduce conflict. It also lowers your stress levels, supports emotional wellbeing and allows you to form better relationships.

Developing your femininity will allow you to tune into the non-verbal communication of emotions and intuition, as these are natural feminine traits. Emotions are energy in motion and affect how we relate to others. Emotions are significant and act as messengers. It's our job to listen and understand what they have to say. For example, anger relates to boundaries, and sadness is a need to let go of something. Emotions help us shape our authenticity and are an imperative and integral part of communication. There's a vast difference between what we're feeling inside and the ability to express it to the outside world.

Communication with self and others is how we unlock and free this division inside ourselves. Learning the language of emotions or emotional granularity is key to having the ability and know how to translate and express the words we're feeling.

For more information, please see my Empowered You Online Programme at FeminineEmpowermentAcademy.com.

Intuition, another feminine trait, is our instinct about whether something feels right. Have you ever felt like you should be doing something, not actioned it and then regretted it? For example, recently, I was a passenger in a car in England. We set off, and my intuition told me very clearly that we were on the wrong side of the road, but instead of acting on it and speaking up, I sat there trying to work out what side of the road we should be on. In the meantime, a car came around the bend, and we had a very near head-on collision. Instead of waiting for my logical brain to work things out, my intuition told me automatically we were driving on the wrong side of the road. Or when you think of someone and then they ring you? Your intuition is kicking in, trying to communicate and tell you something. Learning to work with your emotions and intuition as tools will give you greater insight and make your communication more effective.

Please go to the exercise below to discover how to start consciously working on your communication skills.

Exercise 10 - The FACTS of Effective Communication:

Effective communication takes practice, but it is worth it to reap the rewards of reduced conflict at work, at home and socially. It can significantly lower your stress levels to be a calmer person, support emotional wellbeing by understanding how to manage your emotions and form better relationships with yourself and those around you.

Below are what I call the **FACTS** of effective communication. Familiarise yourself with them and practise them in your next three conversations:

- **F**ocus on what others say; pay attention.
- **A**ctively listen to what others say instead of thinking about what you will say.
- **C**onnect with the person you're communicating with. Use compassion; it's not all about you. What's going on with them?
- **T**une into the nonverbals - tone, body language, and emotions.
- **S**how interest in what others say and respond accordingly rather than waiting for your turn to speak.

In your journal, note how it felt to focus on the above **FACTS** of effective communication. What differences did you notice?

AFFIRMATION

I am Communication

CHAPTER 10

Time to Give Yourself a Good Talking To

How do you speak to yourself? With compassion and understanding? Or are you like the majority of humans who talk to themselves terribly?

"You stupid idiot - why did you do/say that?" Or "What's the point? Or "Why bother trying? You know it won't work" the voice in your head says.

We're all familiar with it, but have you ever considered what you're doing and the damage it may be causing? No, I didn't think so.

This code breaks communication down into self-talk and communication with others, exploring the differences and why it's important for you to be consciously aware of both. Communication is a key factor in being your authentic feminine self. The way you communicate with yourself and others is the process that conveys and confirms your thoughts and beliefs. You see, words are spells. What we say or what others say to us can greatly impact our thoughts, emotions, energy, beliefs and actions. That is why you must be aware of what you are saying to yourself. It still has the same impact, whether in your head or out loud.

Self-talk – how you communicate with yourself – is a big deal. It is your internal dialogue, often automatic and unconscious. The inner voice you hear berating you, calling you names and putting you down is - YOU. Your inner voice combines your conscious thoughts and unconscious beliefs to create your self-talk. If you talk to yourself in a critical and demeaning way, you are programming yourself to think and act negatively.

Phrases such as "Oh, I'm so rubbish at doing this," "See, I've messed it up again", "It's all my fault", and "I can't do anything right" produce negative emotions and that heart-sinking feeling of failure. This, in turn, leads to low self-esteem and unhealthy behaviour patterns like stress and limited thinking and is also linked to depression. Please note excessive negative self-talk is damaging and adversely affects success. This is very different from the odd bout of self-criticism, which happens to everyone.

Many of us have had external factors unconsciously teach us to think and act like this. Often, it's what we see and hear growing up from our caregivers. It isn't anyone's fault – it just is what it is. But once you become aware of negative self-talk, you can do something about it, regardless of how old you are.

My upbringing was in a very critical household. As an adult in my thirties, I became aware of the automatic negative self-talk I told myself. Statements like "You stupid fool, why did you even think that would work?" were part of my unconscious psyche.

I had to retrain my self-talk to respond with more compassion, kindness and positivity. Gradually, and with lots of conscious practice, I could respond with automatic positive statements like "Well done for trying something new. What have you learnt from this?" Now, in my fifties, I rarely have negative self-talk; if I do, I turn it into something more positive.

By being conscious of how you speak to yourself, you can choose a better approach and create a new positive and very effective habit. Start replacing any negative self-talk with encouragement and kind words. Catch yourself thinking or saying something negative and change it, for example, "You are so stupid, you never get anything right" to "It's okay to make a mistake, that's how we learn, now what will I do differently next time?"

Positive self-talk is a powerful tool. Consciously practising this will boost your confidence and elevate your feelings of self-worth automatically.

Please go to the following exercise to learn how you rate your self-talk and learn strategies for improving it.

Exercise 11 - Self-Talk

Be honest; how is *your* self-talk?

Please rate it here by placing an x on a scale of 1 to 10 below - 1 is extremely negative, 5 is half negative and half positive and 10 is extremely positive:

1-----------------------------------5-----------------------------------10

Commit to improving your self-talk by practising awareness of your self-talk and promising to improve it by being more positive, for example:

Instead of saying, "Typical, I got it wrong again", you can say, "That was difficult, but I gave it my best shot, and now I will be better prepared if it happens again."

It is important to take responsibility for your part without destructively attacking yourself.

Another useful tool is to swap 'I' for your name, which distances you away from the self. The above example would look like, "(Your name), you gave it your best shot, and now you will be better prepared if it happens again."

CHAPTER 11

Successful Healthy Relationships

There are many different types of relationships. Here, we focus specifically on female/male intimate relationships based on my experience. We all want healthy and successful relationships with a significant other. But what does it take to create them and keep them?

Relationships are like bank accounts – you will encounter difficulties if there are fewer deposits than withdrawals. I had to learn this the hard way, losing a few serious relationships along the way first.

My parents weren't great role models of what a successful intimate relationship should look like. I never saw them hold hands, kiss or be particularly kind to each other. As a family, the six of us existed together in a very practical and efficient way. Everyone knew their role and got on with life in relative harmony but without any touch or positive affirmations. I didn't learn the 'working together as a team' and the 'give and take' aspects of a successful relationship. I believed relationships happened easily and perfectly, like in the movies. You meet someone you like, fall in love and live happily ever after. Somewhere, I had decided this was how it is, which is strange in one way as that hadn't been my experience with my parents.

By the time I married for the first time in my twenties, I'd had two failed serious relationships. The first ran off with another woman, and the second I ran off as he was abusive. I decided to make this relationship all about me. I made the choices and wore the trousers... inevitably, that didn't work either, and we divorced a few years later.

In truth, relationships don't just happen. You have to work at them, and that takes time and communication. Finding out the differences between communication styles and taking time to communicate honestly and authentically with compassion will make a big difference.

Below are the four main communication styles that you may recognise in yourself, family, friends and work colleagues:

Passive - where someone is emotionally dishonest, indirect, blaming, or apologetic.

Aggressive - where someone is inappropriately honest, direct, attacking, or controlling.

Passive-aggressive - where someone is passive on the surface and indirect, but underneath, there's anger and manipulation.

Assertive - where someone is appropriately honest, direct, sensitive to others, and empathic.

It is also important to consider the differences between women and men. We have different needs and might not like to admit it, but it's true. Stay with me here. Women in their feminine tend to need to be validated, and men in their masculine tend to need to fix problems. So, when you are a woman in her overdeveloped masculine, this can rock the boat and cause issues. We can find ourselves in a relationship with a less masculine man, someone we can control, someone who won't cause us too much trouble and who will go along with our ideas and plans.

Women in their feminine also tend to be more caring. Men in their masculine tend to take more risks. Men have an inbuilt giving, providing and protecting desire; women are more nurturing and receptive by nature. You get the picture. A masculine man doesn't want a masculine woman, and a feminine woman doesn't want a feminine man. These are the differences that exist in our primitive souls. It's how we are programmed. In intimate relationships, we look for a spark that clicks for both parties. Without it, the relationship is more of a friendship.

Men and women also have differences in their brains. Dr Brizendine states, *"Men and women have different brain sensitivities to stress and conflict. They use different brain areas and circuits to solve problems, process language, and experience and store the same strong emotion."*

Recognising and accepting these differences as strengths is the key to successful and healthy relationships. Trying to balance both masculine and feminine so that you can draw on whatever response is the most appropriate at that moment is the way forward for everyone. Try bringing more awareness to your problem-solving. For example, ask yourself whether the situation needs patience and consideration or swiftness and action.

More differences manifest in that women need to express their emotions more than men. The more a man can listen to a woman's feelings, the more she will feel safe, heard and understood. She, in turn, is more able to accept and appreciate him and respond with the encouragement and approval he needs, too.

I have now been with my second husband for over twenty years. It's the longest intimate relationship I have ever had. I have changed and grown on our journey together, and so has my husband. Sure, we have disagreements; that's part of life, especially when we're both strong-willed, but we have learned to communicate and agree to disagree or find a middle path.

Our assertive communication skills have been crucial to our long-lasting, compassionate, loving relationship. They help us to talk things through and see each other's perspectives. We have both changed immeasurably since we met many moons ago, but luckily, we've grown together, have lots of shared interests and are each other's best friends.

Although I have been focusing on female/male intimate relationships, this information is also useful for any relationships between men/masculine and women/feminine, whether friends, work colleagues, family or teammates.

Before I finish this section and you do the next exercise, I will leave you with my Top Ten Tips for creating and maintaining healthy and successful female/male intimate relationships:

1. Learn, recognise and respect the differences between men and women

2. Listen actively to what the other person says and does not say (non-verbal communication). Understand first before trying to be understood

3. Talk to each other honestly and openly with empathy

4. See things from the other's perspective

5. Invest time and energy into your relationship

6. Be supportive and compassionate

7. Spend quality time together

8. Share an interest or two

9. Be flexible

10. Have fun

Please go to the following exercise to discover more about creating positive relationships.

Exercise 12 - Successful and Healthy Relationships

Communication is key to any relationship, whether with a partner, a work colleague, a friend or a family member.

As we all have different communication styles, understanding what someone really means and being understood can be difficult and confusing. For example, even though my husband and I speak the same language, I often need to ask him to repeat, in another way, what he has said to me. Our communication differences may frustrate us both, but asking him to repeat and explain in another way is necessary. Then, when I understand, I reflect it back to him and adjust as needed.

What communication style are you?

Does it change depending on who you are speaking to?

Please follow this link to find out which communication style you use, then make a note in your journal of how you can improve your communication and note the communication style you recognise of your friends and family:

https://umatter.princeton.edu/respect/tools/communication-styles

Personal Feminine Empowerment Journey - Communication

A feminine approach to communication has helped me be a leader in a masculine industry.

So, to paint the picture, after university finished and I spent a couple of years travelling the world, I found myself in London, where I spent the next seven years working in corporate advertising in London ad agencies. I loved the 'work hard, play hard' mentality of the industry, and I was definitely taking that mentality to its limits for a long time. My attitude has always been - if I do something, I always give 100%, and even though I loved the social aspect, I always ensured my work did not suffer.

Whilst I loved the high-energy, fast-paced environment of agency life, outside of work I discovered a new passion: yoga. I loved caring for my mind and body and became more self-aware as a female. This helped me to balance the busy, masculine vibe of advertising. Yoga became my real love, and I soon noticed that I was less interested in Friday's boozy lunches or late-night meals and drinks as I wanted to avoid anything impacting my Saturday morning practice.

As my passion for yoga had grown, it had really been more than exercise; it allowed me to tap into a more mindful and softer part of me that I had unconsciously neglected. At this point, I felt truly disconnected from the corporate world. The turning point was when my agency announced they were making cutbacks. However, rather than seeing this as a bad thing, I instantly knew I would take this opportunity with both hands and follow my new passion.

I spent the next three months in India, trained as a yoga teacher and took the first steps in launching my new business - helping other yoga teachers with their marketing! I realised I could harness my skills and experience from the corporate target-driven world and use them to make a difference in an industry where my heart truly was. I saw an opportunity to support friends and businesses in the yoga world who had the same passion as me but needed more skills or know-how to promote their offerings.

I now see the value in my 'masculine' approach to business, helping clients who are so skilled in being of service and more in their feminine mindset that they benefit from my strategic thinking and planning, which was always key in my corporate life. My success stems from this, combined with a large majority of my clients being female, meaning I can really connect with them and see the world of sales and marketing through their eyes.

As I write this five years later, I am an accredited business and marketing coach and the founder of a boutique digital marketing and ads agency, working with leading wellness clients worldwide. Having left London behind, I can do everything from my new home, Ibiza.

Charlotte Reynolds - Business and Digital Strategy Coach

CHAPTER 12

Code 4 - Confidence

What is confidence? What does it mean to be a confident person? Having confidence is about believing in yourself and your abilities. But how do we know if someone is confident?

Usually, we think someone is confident when they appear to know what they're talking about and speak with conviction. Their body language is straight and upright. They make eye contact and give off this air of 'believe me, I know what I'm talking about'. But what if it was a learned technique to appear confident? What if it was fake confidence to make you think they're confident? What if you challenged them? Would they respond kindly, or would they respond defensively and aggressively? Would their self-esteem be so fragile that once triggered, they shatter into pieces in front of your eyes or run off in a huge huff?

You see - confidence and appearing confident is a bit of a minefield. We can go through life meeting people who may or may not be confident but act like they are - indeed, acting the part of a confident person very well. When really it's a cover-up.

Often, these people have low self-esteem and have learnt to act confidently in certain situations to appear better, more interesting and more appealing than they actually think. People with inflated egos often pass themselves off as confident people. Still, truthfully, they're the ones with low self-esteem who constantly try to prove to the world that they are better than who they really are. It's exhausting! I know as I've been there!

At my over-inflated ego's highest point, my ego regarded itself as untouchable and far superior to anyone else. If challenged, I was aggressive, so I often went unchallenged. I acted like this because my self-esteem was low. I wanted to be more than I was. I wanted people to think more of me as I felt I needed to prove to the world that I was superwoman and not your average working mum.

For me now, it's quite unreal to think that I was that person. Don't get me wrong, my ego can still rise to the challenge every now and again, but usually with my level of self-awareness, I recognise what's happening or get challenged and calm my ego down by talking through what's happening for me.

Humans are very complex creatures, and there is much to learn about how we work and many factors that can influence our thoughts and behaviours. Confidence is about being your authentic self - not acting confident or fake, just real, true, authentic confidence. This takes vulnerability. Being vulnerable is a big part of being authentically confident. Being willing to admit you don't know something or are wrong is being vulnerable.

So how do you get to be authentically confident, I hear you ask?

First, be willing to be vulnerable and admit when you don't know something.

Second, start practising being authentically confident by focusing on where your strengths are and what makes your heart light up - the things you truly value in life.

Third, bring some humility into your life. If feeling superior to others comes up for you, try remembering that we are all in this together, each with different lessons and skills to share.

In the next section, you will learn your top five strengths, what you value most in life (besides your family, pets and friends). Practising your top strengths will help you learn how to be authentically confident. For example, my top strength and value is creativity. No, creativity isn't just about painting, drawing and writing; it's also about creating ideas and solutions – fixing problems in an 'out of the box' way. Remember we covered this at the beginning of Part 2. This is something I do naturally ALL the time without even trying. I know I do it very well from results and others telling me so, and I'm very confident at it in a very authentic way.

Are you starting to understand the difference between confidence and authentic confidence? We all have different strengths, and by practising your own often, you will naturally learn how to be authentically confident in these areas. Once you've made it a habit, you can move on to other areas using the same techniques.

It's also important to note here that when practising authentic confidence, it's essential that you fill your own gaps. What I mean by this is that you look to yourself for the bits you're uncomfortable with or afraid of instead of looking outside yourself. For example, if you don't like being alone and always rely on others for company, it's time to try spending time doing something you like on your own. This helps you on your journey to authentic confidence to boost your self-esteem. It's time to start relying on yourself more, your opinion, judgement, choices, etc.

Reflect on your confidence journey. Have you been acting confident as opposed to being authentically confident? Write your answers in your journal.

CHAPTER 13

How to Feel Good About Yourself

No one can take advantage of your insecurities unless you allow them to! This may sound harsh, but it's true. Even when we get manipulated by others, it's our responsibility to watch for the prior warning signs and adhere to them rather than ignore them, even if our ego has other plans.

I am guilty of ignoring warning signs that would have saved me a lot of pain and heartache. I genuinely thought I'd hit the jackpot when I met my youngest daughter's birth dad! He was tall and handsome and wanted to be with me. I ignored the early warning signs that he wasn't a good fit for me. I ended up in a violent, abusive relationship with a guy who constantly lied to me, had a terrible drink problem, a whole host of issues and many convictions.

If I had taken notice of the early signs, like after two dates (I discovered he'd been lying to me, and alarm bells signalled inside my body to run away), I would have saved myself a lot of grief. Still, I ignored my intuition because I thought he was hot, and I was lucky as a single parent to have him.

Looking back, I realise that my self-esteem and self-worth were quite low. I'd just come out of my first long-term relationship and was desperate not to be left on the shelf. I wanted to have more children and create a family, and I didn't want to wait. I literally fell for the first guy that showed me attention.

In our competitive society of more, more, more, so many of us don't feel like we're enough. A lack of self-confidence can make you feel inferior to others and unsure of your opinions, capabilities and worth. We look outside ourselves for validation instead of forming a solid inner relationship with ourselves.

Exaggeration is a natural form of human behaviour. People feel the need to exaggerate their capabilities or experiences and put down others to feel superior. Such people also lack self-awareness but, unfortunately, aren't aware of it. Exaggeration isn't the way to build true self-confidence. It's the way to inflate your ego. Psychologists refer to this as 'self-enhancement bias' often due to low self-esteem and can lead to narcissism.

So far, all the previous chapters in this book have been about laying a good foundation for building true inner confidence to balance your masculine and feminine. Step by step, you have been developing a framework of tools and techniques to understand and practise authentic confidence and feel better about yourself.

Feeling good about yourself is an inside job. It's not just about behaving confidently, which can be an act. It's about building true self-esteem to handle rejection and compliments. Self-esteem is the real deal and creates a lasting and positive impact. The best way I have found to raise self-esteem is to start with self-compassion, as you learned in Chapter 8. Take a moment to check that you've ditched the harsh self-criticism and are now practising positive self-talk.

I may sound like I am repeating myself, but this part about self-compassion is so important that you may want to go back to Chapter 8 and reread it so that you really get it... after all, developing a superpower takes practise. And while you're at it, make a note in your journal about where you're at with your own self-esteem and how you can improve it further.

Learn to connect with and value yourself

Using the tools you have already learnt as your foundation, you will focus on feeling concern and respect for yourself. It is time to treat yourself with kindness; start by intending to be more you by connecting with all parts of yourself. Be aware of your emotions, all of them, and the messages they are trying to tell you.

Recognise and accept your imperfections without judgement. Honour YOUR values and opinions – those that you feel are important to you, not other people, but you. This takes courage and determination - but it is worth it. These strategies help us to feel stronger, more confident and able to act from an authentic place with integrity.

Small changes will happen automatically by putting everything so far into practice from this book. Make a note in your journal about how your awareness has changed. What have you learnt already? How are you reacting differently?

You can never become unconscious again once you are conscious of such information. The awareness is like a magnet, drawing everything together to make you feel good about yourself.

Try this next exercise to establish your own top character strengths;

Exercise 13 - How to Feel Good About Yourself

To be authentically confident, we need to know what really matters to us and what we value in life. Practising self-compassion by being kind to yourself, ditching harsh criticism and honouring your values are brilliant ways to raise your self-esteem and, as such, your authentic confidence. By increasing your self-esteem, you will feel much better about yourself. Self-esteem refers to how much we value ourselves.

If I asked you what you value most in the world, you would probably reply with family, friends and pets. Yes, these matter, but what else really matters to you and makes you, you? Knowing your values can help increase your authentic confidence and boost your self-esteem.

To discover what you truly value in life, take the survey below. The results will give you a list, in order, of your character strengths, those qualities that come most naturally to you and are from what you value in life. Note your top five strengths in your journal and try to include and use them in your daily life to become happier and feel better about yourself.

Top Tip: Focus on one of your top five strengths daily and consciously consider how to incorporate it into your day to make it a habit.

To find out what your character and personality strengths are, follow the free survey link below; it only takes fifteen minutes:

https://www.viacharacter.org/www/#

AFFIRMATION

I am Confidence

CHAPTER 14

The Power of Intuition and Gratitude

Intuition is a gift available to every human being. Although society says women are naturally more intuitive than men, female intuition is an extra special gift. Intuition is that internal feeling you get when something is or isn't right. It draws on your unique experience to create a sense of inner knowing. We can develop this inherent skill by practising to sharpen our awareness and perceptibility. It is real and available to anyone, anytime, anywhere.

Trusting our gut feeling is a well-established business, social and home life skill. For example, have you ever had a thought while driving to work that you should take a different route, and you ignore it, only to find out there's a traffic hold up, which means you end up late into work but could have got to work on time if you'd have taken a different route and followed your intuition?

Research shows that our intuition can help us make better decisions by trusting our innate ability to know what's best for us, which gives us more confidence in our ability to make our own decisions. Yes, I know this sounds woo-woo, but intuition is actually a scientifically backed skill.

People often refer to intuition as a gut feeling or instinct. It's no surprise then to learn that our gut is often called our second brain, with its own information supply, ecosystem and neural network. However, intuition is a gift that many of us do not use. Many people ignore their intuition when making choices and base them on logic, fear, denial or doubt.

I experienced this first-hand in a previous job twenty years ago. I found myself stressed and in need of control over everything around me. I tried to convince myself that all I needed to do in my job was to work harder and smarter, and all would be okay. My intuition told me I was throwing myself into a toxic lion's den daily, with no escape route. I didn't listen. I didn't want to listen as this may have meant I was wrong about my dream job. I didn't want to be wrong. My ego didn't want to be wrong, so I forged on. I chose to squash any intuitive feelings deep down into the unseen pit of my stomach and ignore my instinct. An instinct that was telling me that something was very wrong.

If I had listened, I would have gone to my boss and discussed the situation before it escalated, but I didn't. My new work environment didn't encourage that kind of open discussion. So, I numbed the voice inside, my intuition, with more distraction by working harder and developing a gym obsession. I'd landed my dream job, but within three months, I was 'let go' for having a management style that didn't suit my team. Nobody had ever said this before.

Previously, I'd been told I had an aggressive style and was unapproachable, which my ego quite liked the sound of, but not that my management style was wrong. It was wrong because the formal management training the company had assigned to me never materialised. It had forced me to armour up in this new toxic environment, and it absolutely wasn't working for anyone. I was devastated initially. My dream job - gone. My career was in tatters. However, forty-eight hours later, I felt very different. Once the shock subsided, something started to awaken and speak to me, my sleepy feminine DNA and it has been rising in me ever since. Yes - this is the job I mentioned at the very start of this book!

Over the years, I have learnt through trial and error to live in alignment with my intuition. I allowed myself to consider and hear it; I trusted my inner knowing. I honour my wise feelings and now know not to question them (usually) and risk talking myself into a different, not as successful, plan. I often speak up if I feel that something doesn't feel right. My husband is used to this now and usually listens to what I have to say, but years ago he would ignore it and push on anyway, only to find his way didn't work out, and he had to spend more money or time correcting it. Often, people try to put off or dismiss their intuition, choosing to listen to others instead of their own inner voice.

Intuition is key to showing up as an authentic and confident woman. It is so valuable and something that all women have if they would only spend time seeking and finding.

Try this exercise to discover how to develop your innate intuition skills.

Exercise 14 - Intuition

Intuition allows you to access your inner knowledge without needing conscious reasoning. Creativity is intuition's best friend.

To develop your intuition, pay attention to ideas, insights and feelings that randomly pop up from nowhere. Follow your gut instinct and intuitive guidance, no matter how small or insignificant you may think.

Bring awareness to your intuition. Learning to trust your intuition and taking action will strengthen it, developing a deeper bond within you to your inner knowing without any need to doubt yourself.

For intuition to develop, allowing it to grow is critical; practising the following points allows you to begin a beautiful relationship with your intuition.

* Make time for creativity in your life.

* Don't discount feelings or hunches.

* When asking yourself a question, check with your gut feeling. Does your answer feel right in your body?

* Reflection is intuition's friend; make time for it and journal

* Encourage yourself to be open to your intuition.

An Attitude of Gratitude

Gratitude is the state of being thankful. It is one of the most powerful tools for wellbeing, authentic confidence and empowerment. As the saying goes, develop an 'attitude of gratitude' if you want to improve your life.

According to Dr Robert Emmons, the world's leading scientific expert on gratitude, the feeling of gratitude involves two stages:

1. The acknowledgement of goodness in one's life

And

2. Recognising that some of the sources of this goodness lie outside the self

In the first stage, the idea is that we recognise what we have in our life to be grateful for, like our health, our home, food on our table, etc.

During the second stage, we recognise that we are grateful to our physiotherapist for helping with an injury, the builder who built our home, the farmer who grew the veggies in my fridge, etc.

Science has proven that gratitude increases life satisfaction and happiness and improves physical and mental health. The more we practise gratitude, the less likely we will suffer from depression or anxiety.

Many researchers have studied gratitude; Dr. Emmons and Dr. McCullough have extensively researched the effects of gratitude practices and found that people who focused on gratitude regularly resulted in significantly higher levels of optimism in many areas of their lives.

Practising gratitude helps you to feel better about yourself and your life. This, in turn, creates more authentic confidence.

As well as this, writer and researcher Sonja Lyubomirsky, Author of The How of Happiness, discovered that gratitude increases happiness, too. *"People who are consistently grateful have been found to be relatively happier, more energetic and more hopeful."*

Being grateful works - it's worked for me, helping me feel better connected to myself, others and my environment. This helps me be authentically confident and feel better about myself. Every morning, I take time just before I get up to tell myself what I am grateful for.

Regular practice is necessary to create a habit as with all these techniques. And remember that the more you practise, the more benefits you'll experience and feel in your life.

Please try the following exercise to learn how to develop an attitude of gratitude.

Exercise 15 - An Attitude of Gratitude

To start developing your 'Attitude of Gratitude', write three things you are grateful for in your journal and see how it makes you feel.

Take a few moments to reflect on three things you are grateful for right now; they can be ordinary (being able to read) or extraordinary (being able to scuba dive). It is totally up to you.

Now, put your pen down and take a few moments to reflect on how this makes you feel.

What is coming up for you as you reflect?

Writing a weekly gratitude list in your journal will help you feel happier, more confident and better connected to life.

Every morning before I get up I compile a mental gratitude list and give thanks for the day ahead.

Personal Feminine Empowerment Journey - Confidence

Growing up, I was painfully shy. For a long time, my insecurities felt like lead weights. It was difficult for me to look people in the eyes or even finish a sentence, let alone say what I really meant. I was uncomfortable in my body and had no confidence in my voice or that what I had to share was of value.

At eighteen, I left home and started working full-time on sailing boats, living and working for months on end with a mostly all-male crew. I felt I was always trying to prove myself. It was exhausting. I wanted to be 'one of the boys', and somehow felt like my femininity was a weakness.

Looking back, it's always easier to connect the dots - I remember getting horrific period pains and being too ashamed even to tell the crew, pretending I had a stomach bug instead.

I was so disconnected from my body, my cycle and my femininity, and it wasn't long before my body started shouting at me. The monthly pain started to get worse, as did my digestion and mental health, leaving me feeling more uncomfortable in my body and mind than ever before.

I left the boat I was working on and took a few months off, diving deep into my very novice Yoga practice and slowly getting to know myself. The journey home to my body - learning to feel, listen and trust myself, began to shift everything. I began to feel more at home within myself. I was learning to care for myself, to respect and love myself through simple practices of listening in and being mindful.

Learning to befriend my body also meant understanding my cycle, my hormones and what my body needed as a cyclical human. I stopped punishing myself for not being 'productive' and social every day of every month for wanting days of rest and time for myself. I stopped comparing myself to those around me and started trusting and acting on how I felt. The more time I spent in meditation, the more I began to observe my insecurities as the fears of being misunderstood and not being enough.

As I studied and started to share the practices of Yoga, I felt a very honest sense of purpose awaken inside of me. Of course, there were moments of insecurity and doubt, but I could feel something deeper within myself that told me - this was right. Being able to trust in this gave me more confidence than ever before. The more grounded I became in this trust - trust in myself, my body, my intuition, and my path; the less concerned I became with what anyone else thought, the less I had to compare myself with anyone else. I didn't have anything to prove or anything to be other than myself, and I felt more confident and in alignment.

Today, I am a qualified Yoga Teacher, leading classes daily. I embrace public speaking and owning my version of confidence.

Daisy Jane Veale
Yoga Teacher

CHAPTER 15

Code 5 - Care

This code is all about care - not the kind of care we have for others but the care we have for ourselves. This can be a strange concept for a lot of people. We are used to caring for others, especially as women and often put others first - partners, children, parents, friends, work colleagues, pets... the list goes on. But what about you?

The kind of care I am talking about isn't necessarily the beauty kind that many automatically think of around 'self-care', like having a facial, pedicure or your hair done (even though it's nice to be pampered). I mean the kind of care that is taking time out of your day, every day, to relax, read, meditate, draw, or listen to music. Whatever it is that helps you to recharge and look after yourself.

Daily self-care is not a luxury; it's vital for a healthy, balanced life. Ask yourself how much care you give yourself. Take a moment to reflect here and write the answer down in your journal.

Boundaries

Boundaries are a huge part of effective care for yourself. It's actually impossible to have self-care without healthy personal boundaries; they are crucial and influence everything. This includes identity setting - consciously thinking and practising how you want to be and how others see you in this life. It makes boundaries a vital part of life and The Feminine Codes book.

Most people don't realise it, but they have barriers instead of boundaries and do not know what healthy boundaries are. Boundaries are personal guidelines: what does and doesn't feel okay to you. Having clear personal boundaries is essential for a healthy and happy life. You need to identify yours, know your limits, and learn how to say "no" when you don't want to do something, knowing that it's okay to say that.

For the longest time, Sarah, my client, gaslighted herself over what felt right for her. Many people in Sarah's life tried and usually succeeded in influencing Sarah's thoughts and actions. Feeling guilty became the norm for Sarah, so much so that she found it very challenging to follow her own feelings of what felt right for her and what didn't. Sarah convinced herself she was too sensitive and not robust enough to trust her feelings.

If you don't learn to set boundaries, people will help themselves to your energy and drain you without you even realising it. We all have different personal boundaries. Some are unique to our experiences, and some we may share with others. Some people violate our boundaries. Have you ever felt like your batteries are totally flat after speaking to someone? Like your energy has just gone, and they have sucked it out of you. These people are energy vampires. They will drain you unconsciously or consciously.

This happens when you have weak or non-existent boundaries that allow you to become invaded. You find yourself giving or leaking too much of your energy, leaving none for yourself, making you feel exhausted and empty. Ironically, the energy vampire feels energised. Weak and wobbly personal boundaries are one of the top causes of energy loss. We deplete and lose our energy when we do things we are not okay with. By contrast, creating strong and healthy boundaries will help keep you fuelled with your energy, feeling confident and valued. It is important for you to identify your own boundaries, know where your limits are and learn how to say "no" or "let me think about that" when you don't want to do something, knowing that it's okay for you to say that.

This is exactly what Sarah did and within months was saying "No" confidently without explanation. No is a full sentence and doesn't need any explanation.

When forming healthy boundaries, you may find that those who influenced you may react in various ways at first, but know that it will pass and continue anyway. The vampires will retreat, and you will step into your power, feeling more in control and aligned with life. Keeping our boundaries maintained needs to be a constant habit. If you haven't got into the habit yet, this is the time to change that. After becoming aware, start putting some firm personal boundaries in place – and remember to practise them by sticking to them.

Examples of positive boundaries:

It's okay to say "no".

It's okay to take time to think instead of saying "yes" straight away.

It's okay to get upset.

It's not my responsibility to fix other people.

It's not my responsibility to please everyone.

It's okay if I don't like someone.

It's not okay to have negative self-talk.

I am entitled to my opinion, which doesn't need to be the same as others.

Try learning how to set some healthy boundaries by doing the next exercise.

Exercise 16 - Creating Personal Boundaries

Below or in your journal, list three personal boundaries you would like to work on. They need to feel realistic and attainable right now for you. Define what is and is not okay for you, such as, 'It is okay for me to say "no" when I don't want to lend my friend money again. Or take her into town when she can get a taxi. Or it's okay for me to sit down, relax, do nothing for thirty minutes and recharge my batteries.'

1 ______________________________

____

____

2 ______________________________

____

____

3 ______________________________

____

____

Commit to your personal boundaries above by promising to uphold them and putting yourself first. This is the only way to maintain your physical, mental and emotional health so that you can help others.

Repeat the three boundaries you've written above often, like affirmations. This way, you will start believing in them, embodying them and making them your reality.

AFFIRMATION

I am Care

CHAPTER 16

The Importance of Self-Care

Every time I travel by aeroplane, it reminds me of self-care. During the safety announcement, flight attendants always tell you that if oxygen masks drop from the panel above, make sure to put your own on before helping anyone else with theirs.

This is self-care. Tending to yourself and your needs first is care for your mind, body and soul so that you have enough energy for life. This enables us to give to others in a balanced and effective way.

I regard self-care as essential. Essential to health, well-being, happiness and general survival. Towards the end of The Feminine Codes, I am introducing the concept of self-care here because you need to have a certain level of awareness from previous chapters and tools before you can start to understand the importance and true value of your self-care.

Even thirty minutes of self-care a day can make a huge difference. Most of us live in a society that tells us to put everyone else's needs first and hands out fistfuls of guilt if we dare to prioritise ourselves. I disagree with this. It's vital to look after yourself before helping others.

How it looks for me is scheduling in 'me time' and replenishing my energy levels often. This means when I need to assist others, I have plenty of reserves to do so. I help people every day, personally and professionally, so it is imperative that I have a habit of self-care. My routine includes maintaining personal boundaries, taking time for myself most days by reading self-development books, spending time in nature, and resting and sleeping well for at least eight and a half hours. I also eat a plant-based diet without caffeine, take regular walks on my own and practice yoga and meditation.

Self-care is different for different people. What I like to do may not suit you. It is essential to find what is right for you. Go to the following exercise and take the quiz to learn which self-care strategies suit you best.

Exercise 17 - Self-Care

It can be challenging for us to schedule time for self-care, but please remember it is essential for your health and happiness. If you don't have enough energy for yourself, you will get sick and tired, physically, mentally and emotionally, leaving you unable to look after anyone, including yourself.

Top Tip: Are you over-committing yourself to others? Do you really want to do that thing, or are you gaslighting yourself?

Start saying "no" or "it's not my thing" to half of the invitations you get asked to.

Top Tip: Do something that energises you - dancing, yoga, walking; find something that you really enjoy and not because you think you should.

Top Tip: Create an equal balance between time for yourself and others.

Please click on the link below to take a self-care quiz created by Berkeley Wellbeing Institute, where you can learn which self-care strategies are best for you:

https://www.berkeleywellbeing.com/well-being-survey.html

CHAPTER 17

How to Love Yourself

Who do you love? Please take a moment now to write a list in your journal of all the people you love. Where on the list were you? Did you even appear on your list?

Remember this: YOU are the most important person in YOUR life. Fact.

All of the techniques in The Feminine Codes are tools designed to help you create a better relationship with yourself and the world around you to maintain balance.

In Part 1, you explored Clarity, your femininity, and what that means to you. Code 1 introduced you to the importance of Creativity. Code 2 revealed to you the superpower of Compassion and how you can use it to benefit your life.

Code 3 made you aware of the impact of Communication, self-talk and how you speak to yourself. In Code 4, you learned how to build real Confidence for yourself. We finish this code, number 5, focusing on Care and specifically the vital topic of self-care, before moving on to the next code, Connection and ending with the final code of Collaboration.

Everything we have covered so far feeds into the culmination of this section - How to Love Yourself - helping you to bring together everything you've learned. Start putting it into practice, and the combination creates a solid foundation for self-love, happiness, authenticity and balance.

Like the oxygen mask analogy in the previous self-care section, I wholeheartedly believe that you need to love yourself before you can truly love anyone else. Loving yourself starts with acknowledging the importance of yourself and then accepting yourself as you are right now. There isn't anyone else the same as you. You are unique. Remember, it's a privilege to be alive; don't take it for granted. Once we mature as adults, we become responsible individuals, unique in our own right. We're ready to discover who we really are and are ready to love.

As Oscar Wilde said, *"Love is a wonderful thing."*

Learning to love yourself is the most wonderful thing ever. No one can take that love away ever, but you. The feeling is one of precious completion and connection. It's a feeling that can be yours forever - a beautiful gift.

"The less you love yourself, listen to yourself, and understand yourself, the more confused, angry and frustrating your reality will be. Your relationship with yourself is the most defining factor in shaping the kind of life you live."

This is a great quote by Lachlan Brown from a very helpful online resource about how to love yourself - https://hackspirit.com/how-to-love-yourself/

Loving yourself is not always the easiest thing in the world, but it is the most important. Please try the following exercise to discover more about self-love.

Exercise 18 - How to Love Yourself

"Loving yourself may not be the easiest thing in the world, but it is the most important." Belinda M Clarke

What three things do you love about yourself? Please write them below or in your journal. They can be physical, practical or character traits.

1 ______________________________

____

____

2 ______________________________

____

____

3 ______________________________

____

____

Now go to a mirror, look into your eyes and repeat these three things to yourself; please include some feeling in your words to make it stick more. Repeat the mirror exercise daily and smile while saying loving words to yourself. Yes it may be difficult at first but keep repeating and honestly it gets easier.

Personal Feminine Empowerment Journey - Care

I could have been a professor at a university, a top journalist for German television, a successful manager of a publishing company in Japan, a spiritual leader, a top therapist, and a few more exciting success stories of a woman born in Germany in the 1950s. I could also have been the mother of a child of mixed race, half German and half Japanese!

Now, I live in Ibiza as a happy and fulfilled therapist and look back to my beautiful, adventurous and exciting long life in which men and love affairs have always played a very significant role in major life-changing decisions.

At the beginning of my career, the academic lifestyle at a German university drew me. However, instead, I decided to follow an Italian lover to India. I became a passionate disciple of Osho, an outstanding master of life and love. In his ashram and commune, I trained as a hypnotherapist, working successfully in a clinic for drug addicts in the Netherlands, feeling fulfilled by helping people give up their addiction. But then it was interrupted by another love affair that led me to a commune life in Germany with a man I felt I'd met in a previous life.

Later, I abandoned a thriving and promising journalism career in Munich for my English partner, who could not bear my intense work life; we moved to Mallorca. While living in Japan and about to become a publishing company partner, I also dropped that opportunity. I left the company to teach and became pregnant by a Japanese lover. I wanted the child, and as the man did not share that wish, I significantly suffered whilst deciding to have an abortion, which lingered on afterwards.

Then life took me to an island in Spain where I found my GREAT love and spent many happy years with him, raising his kids, making his house into a home, and helping his company thrive and succeed. I was delighted as his other half and admired by many friends for our happy and loving relationship until he fell in love with a young woman, and we had to split up. I left behind the man of my dreams, my house, belongings, job, kids, and identity. I felt less than half, like a used handkerchief thrown in the bin. Therapy helped me avoid my acting on the suicidal moments.

Life had mercy on me, and I accepted a job offer on a small island nearby and rose slowly, slowly, very slowly from the ashes like a burnt phoenix. I had put the care of everyone else before myself, following men for love and existing on the leftovers without paying attention to my care needs and prioritising them.

It took me almost two years to find out who I was, to find myself without a man by my side whose existence defined me and gave me a place in the world. I discovered what I wanted to eat and when and how (the last partner hated when I ate standing up, so for weeks, I ate standing until it felt just too stupid!), I tried to become a lesbian (which did not work - yet), and I explored what profession was calling me.

Thirteen years later, I fully know myself, love myself and do not need a man to give me a place in the world. For decades, I had felt worthy and loved because one person loved me. Now

I know that I love myself, LIFE loves me, and I love (almost) everybody, spreading my love to many people, men and women, animals and plants, the earth and the oceans. It was a tough lesson, but now I teach other women that they are enough and worthy to receive love even without a man by their side.

Life allows me to teach the power of a kind and loving heart by living in daily gratitude. And I often feel like a rose with a sublime perfume might feel. If there is someone who wants to have a sniff, they are welcome. And if not, the rose is just as happy. What freedom!

Shambala Wegner - Life Coach and Heart Mentor

CHAPTER 18

Code 6 - Connection

Connection is a deep psychological need, yet most humans seem unable to connect easily to self, others or nature. Travelling on the tube in London is a great example. No one looks at anyone else, choosing to stare at their phone, book, magazine or media adverts - anywhere but make eye contact with a stranger.

A typical and common masculine trait is not asking for directions if lost. This is again an example of not wanting to connect to people you don't know, strangers, when you're in a vulnerable state. It seems such a contradiction, given that humans are wired to connect. Maybe it's patriarchal societal conditioning convincing us that talking to anyone outside our safe circle of friends and family is scary and dangerous.

Many people hate the countryside, regarding it to be a place of horrid bugs, smells and dangerous plants; yet connecting to nature is one of my favourite pastimes, bringing me joy and filling my heart with a full, warm feeling. I love sitting in nature, listening to the birds and looking at the trees, plants, insects and flowers.

Connection to self is something most of us have to relearn. The word *'person'* comes from the Latin persona, which basically means mask. Although we're born whole and perfect, we learn to wear many different masks early to create personas to act differently in different situations. This makes it incredibly difficult for us to connect to our true selves and, ultimately, others. The skill here lies in our learning persona management, as each mask we wear is a persona. For example, your work clothes belong to your work persona, who you are at work, and by wearing your work clothes, you act accordingly. If you wore your work clothes to attend a friend's birthday, would it influence how you acted? And if you wore your favourite slouchy sweatpants to work, would you behave differently? How would it feel? Would it be confusing for you?

Tara Brach, tells a great story about a guy who is late for work, claiming he got distracted by a clown outside. He is asked, *"Was it a real clown or someone dressed up as a clown?"*

You see, we identify so much with the masks we wear each day that we lose who we truly are and our connection to self. Most of us go through life jumping from one mask or persona to another - accountant, wife, mother, daughter, sister, friend, auntie, cook, cleaner, shopper, chauffeur and so on. We tend to identify as each one and often forget to put them aside, believing this is who we really are.

With awareness, we drop our masks or personas, understanding them to be temporary, not permanent, features of our lives. We can return to the self and who we truly are and reside there, fully connecting to the self. We learn to discard the clutter of the many personas we've acquired, even if only temporarily, to spend time in our true nature. For many people, connection is an abstract concept, and many don't really understand what connection is and how to get it. That is because most people are too busy living life from their many personas or masks and, as such, in their heads to connect to the rest of themselves or anyone else.

This may be controversial, but I understand it to be true. Life experience, not only with my clients, has shown me repeatedly that most people live in their heads. What I mean by this is that their thoughts and general busyness engulf them rather than being in touch with the rest of themselves and feeling what's happening inside and with their bodies. Our heads are where most of us reside - in thought, planning, organising arrangements for work, trips away, or it could be as simple as 'What am I going to eat for dinner?'

The head's favourite pastime is thinking, planning and worrying, and by spending lots of time in your head, that is what you will find yourself doing a lot of. Don't get me wrong, planning and thinking are very useful when done productively and with a positive intention, just not always like an addiction. The more we are in our head, the more disconnected we are from the rest of us - our physical body and our emotional and energetic selves. We create a void between our mental, physical, emotional, and energetic selves. Yes, we are much more than just a physical body; we are also a mental, emotional, and energetic body.

At a recent Osteopath appointment, I amazed myself and my Osteopath by connecting to my pelvis enough for her to adjust this sensitive area easily and for me to feel the release of years of built-up tension melting away. I did this by linking my body-mind connection and sending my focus to my pelvis. Our body-mind connection is incredible.

Most people generally live in their heads. I get it - life is busy and demanding, but this disconnects them from the rest of themselves and their feelings, disconnected from what's happening in their bodies and sensations within themselves. I was there, too, not so many years ago. Most clients come to me in this disconnected state - worried, anxious and overwhelmed where thoughts consume them, overworking their brains. Instead of stopping and questioning what's going on, why and what needs to change before working with me, they insist its normal and continue in a state of overwhelm and stress. They find many ways to distract themselves away from what's really going on.

My client Laura first booked one of my bespoke retreats in Ibiza. She was suffering from the effects of burnout after working for a multi-international company for years. Laura had been doing her best, working harder and harder for a company in a very masculine and competitive environment. Now she was ill; they didn't want to know and were trying to push her out and get her to quit. Laura was very detached from the neck down. Her awareness of what was occurring in her body each day was negligible. She'd lost track of the last time she'd had a period but knew she wasn't pregnant, and she didn't have time for a relationship as work had been her main focus in life. She was exhausted and felt so overwhelmed her head hurt.

After a few days of resting, gentle yoga, sea dipping, nourishing food and healing for her central nervous system, Laura was ready to explore opening herself up to connecting with her heart, body and all the rest of her being. I started gently by getting Laura barefoot on the grass and grounding her on the earth amongst the trees, breathing easily in and out of her belly, not her chest, as I guided her through a short-standing meditation. This helped Laura to connect to her breath, calm her central nervous system and relax. Once in this relaxed state, Laura could move on to accessing a connection with the rest of her body using one of my guided meditations - Head to Heart. This helped her become aware of the difference between being in her head and heart and really feel that difference.

https://feminineempowermentacademy.com/head-to-heart-guided-meditation/

For the first time in as long as she could remember, Laura gradually became aware of sensations in her body and continued practising meditation outside on her own. She also noticed her body reacting to certain foods and drinks in her solar plexus and stomach areas. She started to feel bloated after eating bread and anxious feelings after drinking coffee. She realised these symptoms had been occurring for years, but she'd cut herself off from the neck down and so hadn't been aware. Upon returning home, Laura became aware that she might have food sensitivities and arranged tests that confirmed her suspicions. She realised that by working harder and harder in such a competitive environment, she'd closed herself off, living in her head with constant overwhelm and disconnection from herself, her feelings and her core values.

Her actions had also disconnected her from those she loved and cared about, her friends and family, thinking she didn't have time as her career came first. Laura continued her head-to-heart meditation practice, which helped her balance her nervous system and form a connection with the whole of herself; she said, "It felt like she was coming home to herself." She developed some boundaries for work, including daily maximum work hours. She put into place time to see friends and family and practice self-care.

If you think that you may be disconnected, try this following exercise

Exercise 19 – Head to Heart

Get yourself comfortable, as I am going to guide you on a journey from your head to your heart...

Sit with your feet flat on the ground, with your eyes closed and hands comfortably placed and relaxed on your legs. Take a deep breath in and blow it out through your mouth. Take another deep breath, blow it out through your mouth, and one more in and out. Now breathe normally for you, at the speed right for you, in and out. Place one hand on your heart, and continue breathing in and out.

Take your awareness to the top of your head and allow that awareness to slowly sink down, like liquid gold from the top of your head, all the way down to your heart, where your hand is. Take your time and imagine the liquid gold moving easily from the top of your head through your brain into your jaw, neck, chest, and beating heart. Allow the liquid gold to fill your chest with a light presence. Breathe easily in and out. Breathe into your heart, expanding your heart with this lovely light gold. Feel your chest expand, rise and fall; feel your hand on your heart. Feel the presence of yourself in your body, connecting with your breath, connecting with your heart and connecting with your body. Feel and breathe in and out a few times more, allowing yourself to feel your hand against your clothes near your heart - breathing in and out.

Take a moment here, breathing in and out. And when you are ready, take a deep breath in, release it out and again, in and out. Bring yourself back. Move your fingers and toes and open your eyes.

Take a moment to reflect on how that felt, and write your answers in your journal.

AFFIRMATION

I am Connection

CHAPTER 19

Bonding

One of the reasons why a connection is a deep psychological need for us humans is that our physical system is programmed to produce a bonding hormone called oxytocin regularly. Oxytocin is released into our bloodstream, creating a lovely connected feeling when we hug, hold hands, share moments, or make contact with a kitten, puppy or baby. Even the simple act of smiling triggers a release of oxytocin. Try smiling right now for a few moments and notice how you start to feel.

Oxytocin is also present during and after birth. It helps Mum bond and ultimately connect with her baby and continues to be present for the first few years, connecting Mum and the baby. When the situation is different, and a lack of intimacy with Mum or another occurs, the baby misses out on these vital connections, which can cause issues later in life in forming relationships.

So we've established that connection is important, if not essential, for humans, but other than hugging everyone and cuddling puppies, how can we connect with other humans and benefit from our hardwired hormone oxytocin?

Sharing a common hobby is a great way to connect with others and feel happy. I've worked with my husband on numerous business projects. Still, the one that stands out the most is a volunteering project we founded in Ibiza - Healing Ibiza. No one got paid, yet over one hundred volunteers joined forces to host the most beautiful and high vibrational annual wellness festival, all set in the gorgeous orange tree gardens of a prestigious hotel in Ibiza. Even our dog, Cosmo, found it blissful wandering around calmly and relaxed off his lead, smiling from ear to ear. Every year we raised thousands of Euros to give to charities on the island, and thousands of people visited, many travelling from countries far and wide to attend.

Volunteering appeals to more women than men, maybe because many roles are caring and nurturing, which can be deemed feminine traits. Whatever the reason, it's a great way to share experiences, make new friends and give back to your community. Volunteering places you in situations where you interact with others, focusing on the common good, developing connections and building special bonds.

Healing Ibiza connected people to themselves, to each other, to the natural environment of the venue, to Mother Earth and often to strangers. The annual event changed many people's lives for the better. Oxytocin was present for anyone and everyone by the bucketful on this special day of the year.

A close connection can begin in the most unusual of ways. My husband Toby takes groups of strangers walking around the Balearic Islands for a week or so (IbizaOutdoors.com).

He's done this for many years and guided hundreds of people on what many others have described as 'much more than a walk'. They all begin as a group of unfamiliar people who don't know each other and are from all different walks of life and nations. Every time they end as a group of lifelong friends, they bond by sharing an extraordinary experience and a journey of a lifetime. It never ceases to amaze me how connected some groups become in a few short days.

Another way to strengthen connection is by sharing a pastime with a friend or partner. Toby and I make time to travel together as it's one of our joint hobbies and pleasures in life to visit and explore different countries and cultures. I know that by planning these trips away from home, the everyday conversations such as - 'Have you fed Cosmo?/When is the cleaner coming next?/Is there enough money in the account to pay the rent?/Have you booked the car into the garage?' we get to be present with each other, sharing new experiences, releasing oxytocin, and connecting more.

What can you do in your life to improve and grow connections? Would you consider volunteering for a worthwhile cause you feel close to? Is there a hobby you and your partner or friend can do together regularly?

CHAPTER 20

Emotions

Emotions are another big area we humans ignore or do not get quite right. Learning how to read and effectively translate emotions of self and others is essential for humans to live a happy, healthy, authentic life. Yet, the majority of people still find emotions difficult to deal with and choose to ignore them as if they simply don't exist.

Women tend to be a little more connected to their emotions, but only if they are connected to their femininity. I was watching a reality TV show recently where all the male contestants experienced huge difficulty in understanding and expressing their emotions in any way that wasn't anger.

Growing up, my family didn't do emotions except anger and the odd spat of happiness. I found this incredibly difficult and confusing. Only later, through studying the subject of emotions, did I realise that as a sensitive child, what I really needed to make sense of the world around me was to learn emotional intelligence. But it didn't exist in the seventies. No one knew anything about it, so I frequently cried and got upset, struggling with not having the skills to know what was happening and what to do.

Psychologist Daniel Goleman popularised Emotional Intelligence in the nineties. It is the art of understanding and managing your own emotions. Emotionally intelligent people can share emotions healthily, identify and verbalise emotions, regulate emotions, understand others' perspectives, and show care and concern for others' emotions.

It all starts with emotional awareness - identifying, naming and managing your emotions. However as this subject area is still relatively new in scientific research and understanding, most people still need to learn how to recognise and regulate emotions. Again, we've been conditioned into being disconnected from our whole emotional spectrum. Or connected to only one aspect of it, for example, the negative emotions - anger, fear, resentment or just the positive emotions - happiness, joy or gratitude without full knowledge of what emotions are.

The emotion my parents modelled when I was growing up was anger. I learnt how to get angry and shout very quickly about something I didn't like. Mum and Dad were incredibly skilled at getting cross and quickly verbalising their anger. As such, it wasn't a surprise that I also honed the skill excellently; it became second nature to me. Although it was very confusing as a child when acting out my anger as both my parents would tell me off for expressing it, even though it seemed okay for them. It wasn't until I was in my thirties that I realised it wasn't such a great skill and I could do something about it by changing my behaviour. I realised that I needed to understand more about emotions, what they are for, how useful they are and how to utilise them fully and properly. I got curious and researched the subject of emotions extensively (I went on to create an online course with my findings called Empowered You to help others too, available at FeminineEmpowermentAcademy.com).

What I found was that change doesn't happen overnight. I'd had thirty-plus years of reacting to anger by getting cross and shouting (a big sorry to my daughters). Learning a new way of reacting and forming new habits would take time. I started to learn that emotions are really useful tools and how important **all** emotions are. Emotions can help us to understand who we are and how to translate the messages they bring us. I changed my mindset by embracing all my emotions and listening to what they were trying to tell me.

We are interaction-based organisms. Understanding how to interact with our own and others' emotions is part of our human make-up. Naming and talking about emotions should be the norm for all growing up and not just a few select phrases like "There's no need to cry", or "Where's my happy little princess?" or "Stop moping and pull yourself together", which instil negative beliefs for life like crying isn't a good thing or I can only be happy.

Karla Mclaren is an emotional expert; she emphasises the importance of storytelling, playing and talking about emotional situations to intentionally create a healthy emotional environment. In one exercise, Karla asks you to look around your home environment and check in to see if it emotionally supports you with everything and how it is displayed. For example, consciously ask yourself how you feel about your living room. Does it feel inviting, comfortable and relaxing?

This may sound a little crazy and woo-woo - but emotions are messengers that try to tell us messages that get sent to your brain to inform you that a change of state is occurring in your body and an action or reaction is needed. It's actually a really cool system that, once understood and practised, is a game changer for life. Let's take anger. This emotion manifests as a reaction to a thought or action. Anger is a message that tells you that someone has crossed your boundaries and something has happened that's not okay for you. Knowing that the emotional system has been alerted and you must take action is very useful. At this point, someone with emotional intelligence who understands their emotions and translates the message will pause and consider their options. Someone without that connection to their emotional intelligence will run away or explode. Most people run away from emotions, avoiding them at all costs or exploding like a firework as an overreaction. This stems from our limbic brain's automatic flight or fight response system.

It's this connection to your emotions that reside in the feminine, using care, consideration, curiosity and nurturing to develop your emotional intelligence skills and thus clearly understand and manage your emotions. Without a connection to self, others and emotions, you're likely to lack confidence in your own decisions, look to others for validation and avoid dealing with negative situations effectively.

Remember your value strengths from Chapter 11? Take a look in your journal and remind yourself of your top three. Living a life connected to your top value strengths will automatically connect you to yourself. How can you ensure you include your top three in your daily life and benefit from more connections?

Personal Feminine Empowerment Journey - Connection

My isolated and disjointed younger years taught me to wear mental armour, push down feelings and adopt a more masculine approach to survive my environment. Underneath the angry, sullen exterior was a softer, feminine me who discovered the power of writing, self-expression and reading. I possibly spent more hours with my head stuck in a novel or a pen fixed in my left hand outside of school hours than most teens you'd meet! This became my firm connection, friend and ally, and we built a beautiful relationship that saved my life.

When it felt impossible to communicate with others around me, I connected to the characters, forging a sense of belonging through the pages of my latest paperback. When I abandoned myself, I found solace through the words that formed on a page in my diary. My writing habit developed into stories and poetry designed to connect with others through emotions and feelings.

I craved deep connection when starved of it. Recognising that you have lacked something vital can be the greatest teacher towards fulfilment. The desire to belong saw me seek other relationships with like-minded souls, even if we lived thousands of miles apart. I was drawn to other empaths, preferring a gentler, kinder and more accepting spirit.

The birth of my son was not only love at first sight, but it opened up a whole new world of belonging. To be responsible for and love the little bundle of joy touched every segment of my heart, and we formed the most magical eternal bond. It was beautiful connecting with other mums as we navigated parenthood. We compared our concerns and funny stories of potty training and weaning – reassured we were in this new life together. The fun trips out and watching our little ones play together, whether feeding farm animals or building sandcastles at the beach – we all were part of one big family sharing our treasured moments.

I took my desire for meaningful connection and used it purposely to support other parents of children with eating disorders – we formed an incredible bond as I gave back through my experiences of addiction – the ultimate form of disconnect. I picked jobs intentionally, and a connection was the driving force as I landed myself in supportive, nurturing, charitable roles. Facilitating inclusive activities, advocacy and running art groups for vulnerable people was a blast and dressing up and handing out Christmas presents as a thirty-something Mrs. Claus was one of my finest career moments!

Eventually, the published word became my best friend. I reached many hearts by connecting souls as the source behind everything I do, as no one should feel alone. Moving to live by the sea fulfilled my soul's desire for a deeper connection to nature and the ocean, enhancing my relationship with self-expression.

Some say connection to others is the most crucial thing in life, but before that, it is the connection to self. We share that person with the world when we know who we are.

Samantha Houghton, Ghostwriter and Book Coach

WOM

CHAPTER 21

Code 7 - Collaboration

Collaboration is the seventh and final code in unlocking The Feminine Codes. Collaboration is the culmination and combination of all the previous codes laid out and explained throughout this book. By collaborating with others, you utilise all the earlier codes of Creativity, Compassion, Communication, Confidence, Care and Connection.

Collaboration is the art of joining forces to achieve a common goal. This is a feminine trait. The masculine counterpart to collaboration is competition. Competition is a natural part of a patriarchal society. Most of us need to learn collaboration as competing is constantly exhausting, and sometimes competition is simply not the right fit for the situation.

Learning to collaborate to achieve a common goal was challenging for me. Like many people, I was very competitive. I am one of four siblings; we competed against each other growing up… 'He's got more chips than me!' 'How come she's got a new toy?' 'Why is he allowed to stay out later than me?' etc. At school, we are encouraged to get higher marks on spelling quizzes than our classmates, to run faster in sports, and to do more homework to get ahead - competition is everywhere in life. At work, colleagues compete for the best desk/office/seat/promotion. At home, families compete for each other's attention; to be right, who will get the best piece of cake or the best seat to watch television?

It's okay because if you learn not to compete all the time and learn how to collaborate with others sometimes, you get a balanced mix of the competitive and collaborative in life. This can be easier said than done, as we're naturally competitive and conditioned - think of team sports. So many people enjoy spending a lot of time playing and watching team sports like football, rugby, basketball and hockey. Although people like the competitive edge of team sports, i.e., winning, people are also collaborating in wanting a common goal, to win. This encourages connection, bonding, support and camaraderie, greatly benefiting collaboration.

I love the following example of how, when we are aware, we can use the right tools for the right situation, balancing our feminine and masculine traits authentically and easily. Akin to second nature, with practice, our neural pathways have formed automatic routes for a more appropriate response.

My husband has an outdoor activities company in Ibiza. His guides are passionate and professional, guiding individuals on amazing walks, hikes, e-bike rides and kayaking tours all over Ibiza's beautiful land and sea and neighbouring islands. They work incredibly well as a tight unit on corporate team-building events, collaborating to get the job done to the highest standard. Yet they also love competing against each other for the best review on social media and online review sites.

Regarding collaboration, creativity helps you pool ideas with others and stimulate and share resources on a bigger scale than individually possible. Bouncing ideas off others often generates innovative new solutions instead of doing everything on your own. For example, I am writing this section during a collaborative writing hour that I am part of. We meet online twice weekly to share briefly and then write for the rest of the hour. Some writers leave their cameras on, some off. The guide mutes everyone, and we all write whatever we like, knowing that our writing companions are doing exactly the same. The collaborative energy is very real as we hold each other gently accountable. Without accountability, it can be too easy to get distracted, as the washing needs doing, or that phone call needs making, or the cat needs feeding... it works.

When I was too much in my masculine energy, I always wanted to be alone writing. Now I am more balanced in my masculine and feminine, using the right tool for the situation is key. A lot of the time, I write on my own, but sometimes I write with others. Both are different experiences, and both have benefits.

The previous codes - Creativity, Compassion, Communication, Confidence, Care, and Connection fit together like building blocks. Along with Collaboration, they form a solid base of new tools and techniques to practise for a more balanced, authentic life:

Creativity is the perfect foundation to build towards collaboration. Creating ideas that develop into the physical together with others is an enriching life experience. In our collaborative writing group, we use a lot of creativity; verbally sharing ideas helps us get into creative flow.

Compassion helps us to think about different perspectives together to relieve suffering. Sharing these different perspectives with others helps create awareness and open new channels of understanding for the greater good, which feels collaborative and works wonderfully.

Communication thrives in a collaborative environment. By practising effective communication, a group will collaborate as a successful team, enabling a harmonious flow of productivity and efficient exchange of ideas with all members respectfully.

By joining forces to collaborate on a project, people who may not appear confident in other situations show their inner confidence and shine in their expertise. It's always lovely to see someone grow in confidence where previously there wasn't opportunity or the environment needed to be more conducive.

Care is at the forefront when collaborating on a shared goal. You not only care about the subject and goal but also care grows for your team members and a sense of self-care about your involvement. All the caring energy directed at the project and its members combine to produce a really special feeling.

Connection when collaborating builds to form strong bonds between the whole team and subsections of mini groups and individuals. The connection you experience when collaborating hugely benefits health by producing lasting feel-good hormones and emotional connections.

One of my most recent collaborations has been working with my siblings to find and manage the best care solutions for my elderly father. He'd been living independently happily for years, but following the Covid pandemic, he'd become more lonely and frail. Working together as a team of siblings was hard for all of us. Yes, we're brothers and sisters and raised in the same family with the same rules, but that was a long time ago, and we all have developed our own opinions and ways of doing things. We may be relatively close in age (just over six years difference between the eldest and the youngest), but we were never that close as a family. We didn't do much in the way of team bonding. We didn't share a love of team sports. We didn't play team or board games (apart from the occasional game of Monopoly on holiday, where one or more of us would usually cheat anyway). We didn't share hobbies. Our family didn't do teams; we did independent thinking instead. Our parents raised us to be very self-sufficient and capable people. So, when circumstances forced us to collaborate, it was very interesting.

Whose opinion is right? How do four independent, competitive adults, each with their own thoughts and opinions at doing things, three of whom have no qualms in letting anyone and everyone know what those opinions are, work collaboratively as an effective team?

Well, I can honestly say it isn't easy. We found suitable and lovely assisted living accommodation two miles from his existing home: A perfect modern and cosy apartment in a low-rise facility of forty apartments. Dad has all his own furniture and a beautiful sea view. Three days before the big move, he fell and broke his hip while outside. In his late eighties, we thought he wouldn't survive the trauma and surgery, but he did and is doing really well considering his age and medical issues. Finding new accommodation and taking on tasks to enable Dad to move was relatively easy. Deciding who manages his daily living requirements was challenging, as we all have opinions of what is best for Dad. I'm using all my collaboration skills, and we are all communicating and still learning how best to work together as a team.

CHAPTER 22

We're All in This Together

As part of practising collaboration, you will inevitably learn the skill of sharing, too. Again, as we are quite a competitive species, the act of sharing often doesn't come easily or naturally.

My daughter is teaching my grandson the importance of sharing and how to share his toys, food and parents' attention. It's incredible to witness such a great reminder. Over and over again, it's explained to him why he should share. It's a work in progress, but at two and a half, he's getting there, and he will share his crisps with me now, which is lovely.

As we all live on our planet, sharing the world's resources, we must know how to share what we have with others and collaborate. We share the same oxygen, water and energy. Most of us don't live isolated in a bubble independent from anyone else, so it really helps to know how to share and be okay with it. A friend's daughter recently won $100,000 on a reality TV show and straight away chose to share it equally with the runner-up.

A local Ibizan resident and restaurateur I know also owns a farm. His dream is to convert it into a production facility where local farmers can use the facilities alongside each other to prepare their produce for sale, as well as a collaboration of agricultural workshops where farmers get to share their knowledge with others wanting to learn.

As humans, we love forming groups and, from a very young age, will seek out suitable groups of friends that we feel comfortable with. Often, these groups can be viewed as in or out groups by individuals or other groups. Within your group of like-minded individuals, you share common values, stories, goals, perspectives, beliefs and all kinds of things. That is what sharing is; groups can be a great environment to develop this skill.

Sharing features quite heavily in our society and is an important skill to learn, not just regarding physical items. It's also important for your mental and emotional health to learn to share issues and problems as they arise. If you never share your problems and choose to store them deep within, they cause dis-ease and find a way out, usually manifesting a health problem.

By learning to share, children learn how to make and keep friends and cooperate and collaborate with others, which helps when living surrounded by people. Children who don't learn these skills find it more difficult to make friends and socialise the older they get. It's harder to learn once you're an adult as you've had years of not sharing, creating a well-developed habit.

Beth, a client of mine, was an only child brought up by parents who were strict with rules for everything - what time to get up, eat, do chores, go to school, do homework, eat and sleep. One rule was that Beth wasn't allowed to bring friends home, and as she only had a little free time to play or socialise, she didn't bother making friends at school. Beth kept to herself and spent break times alone, reading and staying quiet. She read a lot as this helped Beth escape from the life she felt quite rigid and unpleasant.

When Beth left home to go to University, she found living with other people in a shared space difficult. It all seemed so alien - noises, voices chatting, laughing, singing, there was always some sound almost constantly. At first, she spent a lot of time in her room reading. She didn't know what else to do. Gradually, Beth started to talk with her fellow students and housemates, which was challenging initially. Thankfully, Beth made a great friend, Lucy on the same course and learnt how to share and trust and build a friendship that they both share nearly twenty years later.

It wasn't easy for Beth; she found it all painful and uncomfortable. Young children naturally interact easily with other children their age; it is second nature. So, if others have held you back from such interactions as you grow up, forming such bonds becomes harder.

Try this - take a few moments to write in your journal how you collaborate and share in your day-to-day life. When finished, ask yourself if this feels right for you or if you want to change this in any way.

AFFIRMATION

I am
Collaboration

CHAPTER 23

The Art of Empathy

With all this sharing and collaboration, I need to mention and acknowledge empathy. Empathy - the ability to understand and share the feelings of another, is a wonderful and innate skill that all humans possess. Empathy manifests itself on a scale; some people are more empathic than others. This is changeable depending on awareness and the environment.

We collaborate with empathic people who are similar in some way to ourselves. As in the following example group sharing, we also find ourselves naturally empathetic as humans. We gravitate to people who communicate, look, and speak like ourselves to form bonds with others easily.

Empathy thrives in groups everywhere, often in places and situations that don't appear very empathic. Such as a group of teenage boys hanging out on a street corner may appear intimidating. However, if you were to observe them without them knowing you were there, you would see a different perspective. The group are all immersed in talking about a friend's party - they share common likes, laughing, sharing experiences and stories.

They listen to who's speaking and wait for their turn to share. They support and care for each other as a group.

Even though we may not be aware of it, empathy is everywhere. Most people don't know the meaning of empathy and confuse it with sympathy, which is about pity for another. Empathy is a hugely important nonverbal skill that is celebrated in music and movies with awards all the time all over the world. We appreciate immensely how beautifully these artists communicate emotions and feelings with so much empathic grace.

I like to think that one of the reasons that Ben Howard is so famous and has won so many awards for his music, besides being an incredibly talented musician, is because of his ability to capture and reproduce a plethora of emotions in his music. It connects and conveys beyond words an energy that is rare among anyone.

Karla McLaren believes that *"we are a wholly empathic species"* and that part of our subsequent species development is for everyone to *"become intentional empaths (and) emotionally awake".*

I wholeheartedly agree. We are intrinsically wired for empathy; it makes us who we are - a collaborative species. Now is the time to develop our skill of empathy consciously.

Personal Feminine Empowerment Journey - Collaboration

For a long time, I was a teacher and taught English as my main subject. I loved the dynamic of a creative classroom, exploring literature with the pupils and opening the space with them for long, philosophical discussions across various themes thrown up by whichever text we studied. I wanted my classroom to be somewhere where people felt safe to explore their ideas and share them; I wanted it to be a haven where the rules imposed on them in the corridors and elsewhere could be relaxed to give them space to breathe, to think, to create, to imagine, to collaborate.

It became apparent to me, however, that some saw my approach to my colleagues as rebellious. I didn't fit the prescribed model of a *teacher*. I didn't care about league tables or about competing for grades. Of course, I wanted my pupils to perform to the best of their abilities. However, I also wanted them to know that success and achievement can take many forms with a far greater lifelong impact than battling for A's and B's.

It clearly emerged that the competitive masculine aspect of the traditional model of teaching and learning was not for me – tables, stats, decreed (and mostly false) assumptions about pupils based on their socio-economic background, encouraging unhealthy competition between students and staff. How can anyone thrive and be mentally nourished in such an environment? And then there were the seemingly endless rules, having exactly the correct type of pen, ensuring that students did their top buttons up, kept their blazers on and that ties were straight. While understanding the arguments in favour of uniforms, the rigidity of the details meant pupils were uncomfortable and focussed only on that, whilst the teachers were permitted to dress far more casually. It was unfair, and the imbalance of power felt so wrong. Many pupils had a million worries outside of school that could have benefitted from a more understanding and flexible approach. It all felt driven by the desire for power over others - if you don't conform to the rules, you are unteachable, and it's all your fault.

The diktat imposed on the pupils was in wild contrast to everything in my belief system. It created a masculine top-down power structure that made me uncomfortable and directly opposed to the collaborative nature that I felt harnessed the most positive learning environment. I realised that I would never fit that particular teaching mould. We all learn more effectively when we collaborate and embark on the journey of learning together, and collaboratively shaping a learning pathway means that we gain deeper knowledge that lasts a lifetime. Moreover, it empowers us, gives us ownership of our learning and develops a sense of community. There is collective joy in creative collaboration.

After fourteen years, the urge to change paths became overwhelming. And so, I migrated into the world of theatre – a world wrought with masculine energy. What was I thinking? However, my role is different and has nothing to do with the hierarchical structure of the traditional rehearsal room in the development of a production. My title, Director of Collaboration, is all about co-creation with the people of Wales. I run a programme through the National Theatre Wales called TEAM, the engagement branch of the organisation. Its purpose is to encourage real social change through the arts by flipping the power balance between an arts organisation and the communities we work with. We aim to empower communities to co-create, connect and collaborate to make theatre and art in all its forms together, both with us and each other.

The cultural landscape in Wales is unique because of diverse Welsh communities and working-class voices. It's my job to reach out to communities, learn from them, and shape a programme of work that suits their needs, hopes and ambitions. Through this work, we can ensure that National Theatre Wales tells the stories that the people of Wales want to tell, in the way in which they want to tell them - bringing a nation together as a creative, collaborative community.

Being a national organisation presents challenges, which can present many difficulties to the feminine version of oneself. By their very essence, nations are masculine in that they are competitive, divided and divisive. However, this only pushes me to bang the drum of co-creation and collaboration even louder as an act of powerful feminine resistance.

True collaboration can channel feminine power in its most magical form – it comprises the ability to nurture, harness strength, find collective momentum, and create genuine, long-lasting change.

Creativity is innate within us all; it's primitive – painting together on a cave wall, coming together around a fire to share stories and experiences, playing music and dancing in response. Creativity means connection; in combination, we find collaboration, align the three, and make community, which means togetherness, within which you find your tribe.

Collaboration means finding yourself within others – you find your tribe and discover a sense of togetherness. It can take any shape or form far exceeding your cultural or societal background – creative collaboration is a fundamental part of all our psyches.

Collaboration nurtures us; it keeps us alive; it's what it means to be human.

Naomi Chiffi - Director of Collaboration

PART 3:

Conclusion

CHAPTER 24

Your Unique Feminine Self

By now, you have worked through each code, gathering lots of valuable and interesting new information on unlocking your unique feminine self and creating balance alongside your masculine. Let's recap the journey that you have been on...

You arrived fresh-faced and wondered what your feminine power looked like, how to balance your masculine and feminine and what tools I'd give you to achieve this better state of being.

You started to learn more about feminine characteristics, which ones spoke to you, and the differences between your masculine and feminine sides. You delved into your feminine mindset and created unique and very personal feminine affirmations.

And then I unlocked the first code for you... Creativity. This code was not just about drawing and painting; you discovered that the more you read, the more you realised that the art of problem-solving and sharing ideas epitomises creativity.

And just like that, you were away. Did you make space for a creative corner in your home?

Next, you learned the core qualities of Compassion and why it is such a superpower that can help anyone and everyone to live a better, more balanced life, especially by learning the art of self-compassion. Compassion allows you to tap into and utilise your feminine side deeply, building compassion for others and, for most of you, for the first time, compassion for yourself.

You learned that compassion is about recognising suffering in others but also recognising the suffering in yourself too. This is one of the most important and useful life tools you can ever learn - an absolute game changer for the better. Nelson Mandela reminded us about the power of forgiveness as a force for good. Lewis B. Smedes shared that forgiveness isn't for the other's benefit; it's for our own. How is that forgiveness list of yours looking now?

Then you moved on to the code of Communication and learnt how easy it is to misunderstand what others say to you, even if you speak the same language! Luckily, to solve the confusion, I introduced you to active listening and how to use it for your own benefit. Can you remember the FACTS of effective communication, and are you using them?

You were made aware of your self-talk, how you talk to yourself and about communication in relationships, whether at work, home or socially and how you can develop healthy relationships with effective communication and my Top

Ten Tips. You learned the four communication styles and discovered which one best describes you. How has that changed for you since discovering your style?

You next moved on to the code of Confidence. First, you learnt what authentic confidence is. Not the fake kind that is surface-deep and so shallow that when not in character, confidence isn't anywhere to be found, as it's hiding because it's way too scary to come out and face anyone. Authentic confidence requires vulnerability, honesty and guts, something everyone has when acting from their unique strengths. There was an exercise to find your top five unique strengths and automatically unlock your authentic confidence. You finished this code with an attitude of gratitude. Are you still practising your gratitude list weekly?

Care was the next code to present itself. It is one of the most important codes so far as it introduces the concept of boundaries, what they are, why you should have them and how you can implement those unique to you.

You learned that self-care isn't just about bathing or doing your nails. It's about looking after your energy, not giving too much away, and always having some left in the tank for yourself. You gave yourself the gift of love from that special person in your life... you!

Connection was the next code you delved deep into, discovering that although connection is a human need, we often don't know how to connect fully and easily with those around us. You found out that most people are scared of connection in some way. That's why you learnt how to effectively connect to yourself, others and nature with your heart and not your head. You also discovered emotions and how they're here to help you and not mess you up.

All the codes so far led you to the last one of Collaboration and learning new ways to collaborate instead of competing all the time. Learning what it's like in someone else's shoes and the art of empathy helped you to bring a new perspective to life. A tremendously helpful feminine trait is how to join forces with others in a collaborative way for the good of all.

Your journey to discovering your seven codes and unlocking your feminine power has been one of awareness, a journey to yourself - to shine a light on what was there hiding in the dark. Now that you are more aware of your femininity, continue practising all you've learnt.

Throughout the whole journey, you have also been developing your journaling skills. Journaling is usually tricky initially, but how is your journaling skill now? Are you reaping the benefits of dumping all those continuous thoughts onto paper so they can do their work and process out of the merry-go-round stage?

The above seven codes have not only formed the basis of a solid foundation for your unique feminine self, but also provided you with a new set of tools so that you can now respond appropriately to any situation in the moment, as it occurs with the new techniques that you've learnt here in this book. It's up to you to practise and create the new neural pathways to form your new mindset and truly balance your masculine and feminine for life. The choice is yours.

Connect With Me

If you have felt inspired by this book please hop over to Amazon and kindly leave me a review.

Let's carry on the conversation here:

FeminineEmpowermentAcademy.com

belindaxxxx@gmail.com

Belinda M Clarke - FB, Insta, LinkedIn

Pregnant Punk at 14, Empowered at 50. My inspirational memoir is available on Amazon https://amzn.to/3ryvt3c